Better Homes and Gardens®

Scrapbooking

Everything you need to know to preserve your memories

Better Homes and Gardens® Books
Des Moines, Iowa

Better Homes and Gardens® Books
An imprint of Meredith® Books

Scrapbooking

Editor: Carol Field Dahlstrom
Writer: Susan M. Banker
Graphic Designer: Angela Haupert Hoogensen
Research Assistants: Judy Bailey, Staci Bailey
Copy Chief: Terri Fredrickson
Copy and Production Editor: Victoria Forlini
Editorial Operations Manager: Karen Schirm
Managers, Book Production: Pam Kvitne, Marjorie J. Schenkelberg
Contributing Copy Editor: Margaret Smith
Contributing Proofreaders: Maria Duryée, Diane Doro, Beth Lastine
Photographers: Andy Lyons Cameraworks, Peter Krumhardt, Scott Little
Technical Illustrator: Chris Neubauer Graphics, Inc.
Electronic Production Coordinator: Paula Forest
Editorial and Design Assistants: Kaye Chabot, Mary Lee Gavin, Karen McFadden

MEREDITH® BOOKS
Editor in Chief: Linda Raglan Cunningham
Design Director: Matt Strelecki
Executive Editor, Food and Crafts: Jennifer Dorland Darling

Publisher: James D. Blume
Executive Director, Marketing: Jeffrey Myers
Executive Director, New Business Development: Todd M. Davis
Executive Director, Sales: Ken Zagor
Director, Operations: George A. Susral
Director, Production: Douglas M. Johnston
Business Director: Jim Leonard

Vice President and General Manager: Douglas J. Guendel

BETTER HOMES AND GARDENS® MAGAZINE
Editor in Chief: Karol DeWulf Nickell

MEREDITH PUBLISHING GROUP
President, Publishing Group: Stephen M. Lacy
Vice President-Publishing Director: Bob Mate

MEREDITH CORPORATION
Chairman and Chief Executive Officer: William T. Kerr

Chairman of the Executive Committee: E. T. Meredith III

All of us at Better Homes and Gardens® Books are dedicated to providing you with information and ideas to create beautiful and useful projects. We welcome your comments and suggestions. Write to us at: Better Homes and Gardens Books, Crafts Editorial Department, 1716 Locust Street—LN112, Des Moines, IA 50309-3023.

If you would like to purchase any of our crafts, cooking, gardening, home improvement, or home decorating and design books, check wherever quality books are sold. Or visit us at: bhgbooks.com

Cover Photograph: Andy Lyons Cameraworks

Dinner Can Wait!

Why does scrapbooking consume us like it does? We'd rather be cropping than cooking dinner. We'd rather be shopping for beautiful papers than reading the newspaper. We'd rather be organizing our photos than rearranging our closets. Scrapbooking is a craft that gets into our hearts like no other.

I have a theory or two for why this happens. For one thing, what is more fun than looking at photos of the ones you love? What a great excuse to relive that summer vacation with the kids or think about that day your baby was born. Can you think of a better reason to take that dusty cardboard box of vintage photos, sit down with Grandma, and listen to her tales before you gingerly copy and place each photo on a beautiful paper background? And have you noticed that there is so much talking that can be done as you sit around a table with family and friends making scrapbook pages together? How lucky we are to have such wonderful products available to use—glorious papers, glues that work, beads and glitter that sparkle, stickers and stamps that add color and pattern, die cuts and borders that add shape—there is no end!

In this book we share idea after idea to create unique and clever scrapbook pages. From elegant to silly, from stunning to cute, each page has a personality all its own. We share ideas on organizing, layout plans, photo tips, and more. Then we show you page after page of scrapbooking ideas. We've separated them into three categories: *Make in 30 Minutes, Create in an Evening,* and *Produce a Masterpiece.* In the back of the book are 16 pages of papers, borders, cutouts, and more, ready for you to use on your own scrapbooking pages. We'll show you how to create your own work of art.

So whether you are an experienced scrapbooker or a newcomer to this exciting art, have fun scrapbooking—and don't be afraid to let it consume you! Dinner can wait.

Carol Field Dahlstrom

Scrapbooking is a craft that gets into your heart like no other.

Table of Contents

CHAPTER 1

It's all about the kids!

Kids light up the world, so it's no wonder their photos make some of the most beloved scrapbook pages. In this fun chapter you'll discover some practical ways to show off your kids' photos as well as clever touches to capture the most treasured moments in their lives.

PAGES 26–57

CHAPTER 2

Remembering life's favorite travels

Visiting new places with the people you hold dear is one of life's best gifts. The scrapbook pages in this chapter will help you preserve those special vacation memories as you learn how to put together graphic layouts, create striking headlines, and add unusual trims to make the pages shine with creativity.

PAGES 58–77

CHAPTER 3

Looking back at fond memories

Preserve family history with vintage-looking pages that honor such topics as military service, Grandma's best recipes, and family trees. We'll show you how to make your pages sparkle with buttons, gems, vellum overlays, and more.

PAGES 78–107

CHAPTER 4

Celebrating holidays and special occasions

Special times throughout the year bring a multitude of joys. Capture these precious occasions on scrapbook pages that will bring smiles and wondrous recollections. From Christmas to Easter, weddings to Independence Day, you'll have ideas galore to make your pages celebrate every holiday memory.

PAGES 108–133

CHAPTER 5

Enjoying beloved hobbies and pets

Whether you're an avid hobbyist or a big-hearted animal lover, this exciting chapter will inspire you to create scrapbook pages that reflect your personal passions. Plus you'll discover lots of journaling and composition tips to apply to your own pages.

PAGES 134–155

How to Use this Book

Scrapbooking is a wonderfully contagious and addictive hobby, so if you're new to the craft—get ready for some fun! This book (created entirely of acid-free paper) offers tips and techniques to help you with the basics and inspiration to jump-start your creativity.

To help you during the planning stages, we've categorized each of our page samples by the amount of time that the page or set of pages took to complete. There are three levels of difficulty: Make in 30 Minutes, Create in an Evening, and Produce a Masterpiece. No matter if you're new to scrapbooking or have created pages galore, you can reproduce any of these pages by following the instructions and informational callouts on each page.

make in 30 minutes

Make quick pages with ready-made embellishments and minimal handwork. Even 30 minutes is enough time to make a clever page or two.

Our Kids

WHAT YOU'LL NEED
- 12-inch square of background card stock
- Coordinating 8½x11-inch papers
- ⅛-inch-wide embroidery ribbon and needle (available at fabric and crafts stores)
- Flat buttons
- Thick white crafts glue
- Computer and printer
- Adhesive
- Photos

Surround your favorite kids with blooms using three easy stitches. Before stitching, mark (but do not cut) photo cutout areas. To make the flowers, use a sharp needle and ribbon to make a French knot (see diagrams, below left) for each flower center. Surround each center with five lazy daisy petals, grouping some flowers together and letting others stand alone. Accentuate the photo openings with running stitches around the edges. After stitching, cut out the marked photo areas using a crafts knife.

Glue narrow strips of the accent paper to the outer corners and trim them even with the mat paper.

Create a vertical headline, print on the accent paper, and adhere it to the background. Glue small buttons at the tip of each letter and randomly on the photo mat paper. Let the glue dry.

Carry the yellow accent to the outer edge with narrow strips.

Use a crafts knife to cut out areas for photos.

Add buttons to dress up a plain computer font.

Use running stitches to border photo cutouts.

Use crafts glue to hold buttons in place.

Combine lazy daisies and French knots to make dimensional flowers.

Annē Mae

WHAT YOU'LL NEED
- Papers or photocopies of paper on pages 161 and 163
- 8½x11-inch card stock
- Deep blue paper
- Copier or scanner
- Crafts knife; scissors
- Marking pen; adhesive; photo

Create this page for a photo of your heaven-sent little one and the papers on pages 161 and 163. Use the paper just as it is or reduce or enlarge the elements to suit your needs. To enlarge the background paper on page 161 to 8½x11 inches, enlarge it 102 percent. The frame and journaling box are provided full size.

Photocopy and cut out each shape. Glue the background paper on card stock. Glue the photo and frame onto blue paper and then onto the background. Glue on the journal box. Add journaling.

On page 163, there is also alternate art to use or photocopy, including a journal box, strips of star paper, and star circles. The strips can be trimmed and used as a photo mat. To cover the corner seams, cut out four circles and glue one over each corner.

CREATE THIS PAGE USING OUR EXCLUSIVE PAPERS ON PAGES 161 AND 163.

Use the papers on pages 161 and 163 to create your page.

Select a photo with the baby's eyes looking up toward the angels.

Separate the painterly papers by mounting the top mat on solid blue.

Choose a banner from page 163 to record pertinent information.

28   29

Include a few handmade touches to give your scrapbook pages extra pizzazz. We'll show you simple tricks to make your photos extra-special.

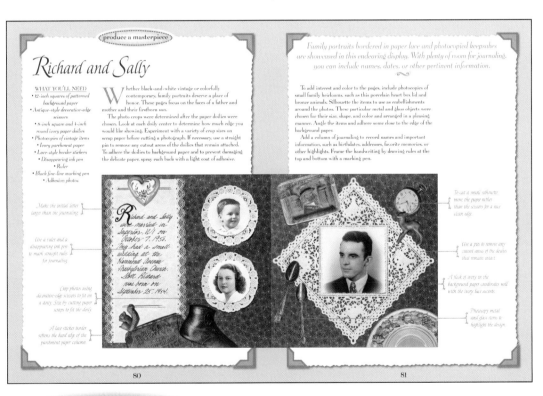

Richard and Sally

WHAT YOU'LL NEED
- 12-inch squares of patterned background paper
- Antique-style decorative-edge scissors
- 8-inch square and 4-inch round ivory paper doilies
- Photocopies of vintage items
- Ivory parchment paper
- Lace-style border stickers
- Disappearing ink pen
- Ruler
- Black fine-line marking pen
- Adhesive; photos

Whether black-and-white vintage or colorfully contemporary, family portraits deserve a place of honor. These pages focus on the faces of a father and mother and their firstborn son.

The photo crops were determined after the paper doilies were chosen. Look at each doily center to determine how much edge you would like showing. Experiment with a variety of crop sizes on scrap paper before cutting a photograph. If necessary, use a straight pin to remove any cutout areas of the doilies that remain attached. To adhere the doilies to background paper and to prevent damaging the delicate paper, spray each back with a light coat of adhesive.

Make the initial letter larger than the journaling.

Use a ruler and a disappearing ink pen to mark straight rules for journaling.

Crop photos using decorative-edge scissors to fit on a doily. Size by cutting paper scraps to fit the doily.

A lace sticker border softens the hard edge of the parchment paper column.

Family portraits bordered in paper lace and photocopied keepsakes are showcased in this endearing display. With plenty of room for journaling, you can include names, dates, or other pertinent information.

To add interest and color to the pages, include photocopies of small family heirlooms, such as this porcelain heart box lid and bronze animals. Silhouette the items to use as embellishments around the photos. These particular metal and glass objects were chosen for their size, shape, and color and arranged in a pleasing manner. Angle the items and adhere some close to the edge of the background paper.

Add a column of journaling to record names and important information, such as birthdates, addresses, favorite memories, or other highlights. Frame the handwriting by drawing rules at the top and bottom with a marking pen.

To cut a small silhouette, move the paper rather than the scissors for a nice clean edge.

Use a pin to remove any cutout areas of the doilies that remain intact.

A flash of ivory in the background paper coordinates well with the ivory lace accents.

Photocopy metal and glass items to highlight the design.

80   81

Go out on a creative limb and make your pages unbelievable works of art. We'll give you ideas that will set your work apart from the rest!

Our Exclusive Papers

CREATE YOUR OWN PAGES USING OUR EXCLUSIVE PAPERS ON PAGES 161-191.

To reproduce pages like those in this book, we give you a list of supplies, instructions, and tips to ensure your success. The highlights and unusual techniques are provided as callouts, so you won't miss a beat.

For added inspiration, we've provided some wonderful designer acid-free papers, borders, and cutouts on *pages 161–191*. You can use them as we have throughout the book or incorporate them into your pages as you wish. The pages are perforated and may be taken out of the book and used as is, or they may be photocopied as you wish. You can enlarge or reduce the pages to fit your scrapbook size. To follow our designs for standard size scrapbook pages, we've provided the percentages used if the provided papers need to be resized. The pages that have been created using these special pages include a diamond symbol (see the symbol at *left*) so you'll know at a glance that you have the art elements for that page in hand.

To get started with scrapbooking and photography basics, see the next page.

where do I start?

If you're new to scrapbooking, all it takes is a little knowledge of the terminology and tools of the trade and you'll be photographing, cropping, and scrapping like a pro in no time. Enjoy an overview of the process on the pages that follow. We'll introduce you to the supplies, terms, and tools that will get you started. Plus you'll get tips from the pros—designers, photographers, and artists—to help you along the way. Then get ready for dozens of incredible scrapbook pages to guide you in creating your own works of art. Once you have a little hands-on experience in the craft, you're going to be hooked— we guarantee it!

Jump Right In

For someone new to scrapbooking, getting started is the biggest hurdle. The best advice? Jump right in! OK, so maybe it's all just a little intimidating. We know. Probably at home you have boxes, bags, and envelopes full of memorabilia and photographs that span years. Where do you start?

To add to the confusion, just visit any scrapbooking store. You may feel you need a degree in design when you peruse the ever-growing assortment of supplies ranging from templates and papers to paints, stamps, die cuts, stickers, marking pens, and oodles more. But don't despair. By reading the next few pages, following just a few tips, and learning some scrapbooking secrets from the pros, you'll be turning out wonderful scrapbook pages in no time.

Scrapbooking papers

Gather Your Supplies

Adhesives

The popularity of scrapbooking means there are lots of helpful products to preserve your memories. Because the purpose of compiling a scrapbook is to preserve memories, use supplies that protect your precious photographs and memorabilia. Purchase a basic list of supplies to give you the confidence and tools to start. We suggest beginning with these items:

- Album and page protectors
- Card stock (white and colored) and other scrapbook papers
- Adhesive
- Black pen (such as Zig, thin and thick tips)
- Straight-edge scissors
- Paper cutter
- Container for organizing photos and negatives
- Storage boxes or bag for supplies

Scissors

Choose archival supplies such as, acid-free and lignin-free paper, acid-free or pH-neutral adhesives, and permanent, fade-resistant inks and pens. If these words are new to you, consult the glossary on *pages 12–15*.

Choose a photo album that contains acid-free pages, or purchase acid-free sheet protectors and slip them into a three-ring binder. Be sure the sheet protectors are polyvinyl chloride-free (PVC-free) or chemically stable; look on the packaging for a "photo-safe" or archival notation.

Adhesives to secure paper and elements to the album pages come in many forms and include photo tape, photo corners, double-sided adhesive dots, squares or strips, glue pens, glue sticks, nonpermanent glue, and bottled glue. Like all of the materials used for your album, the adhesives must be acid-free. You may wish to keep several types of adhesives on hand, because certain adhesives work better for certain applications.

Optional supplies to enhance your scrapbook, mat your photos, and create interesting backgrounds include acid-free precut mats, borders, and specialty paper. Acid-free permanent markers and pens in colors assist you with decorative writing and are fun for adding doodles to your scrapbook pages. Use decorative-edge scissors to cut your photos into interesting shapes and crop unwanted areas.

Other supplies you may want to consider are stickers, templates, decorative rulers, paper punches, rolling ball glue pen, rubber stamps, computer clip art, corner rounders, stencils, and a circle cutter.

Scrapbooking is an adventure, so share it with friends. Besides enjoying the opportunity for a get-together, it's the perfect chance to share supplies.

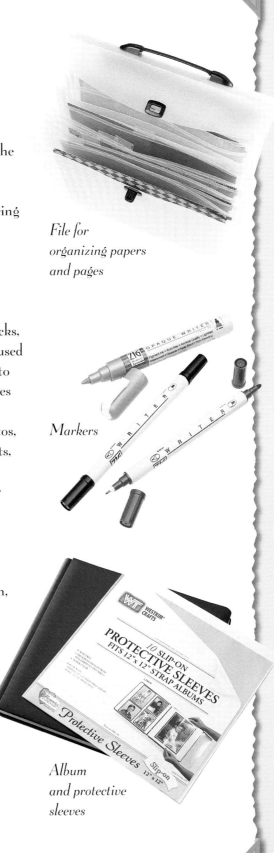

File for organizing papers and pages

Markers

Album and protective sleeves

Scrapbooking Glossary

Haven't heard words like these since high school chemistry? Here's what to make of scrapbooking terminology.

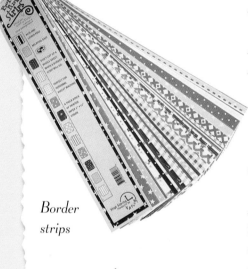

Border strips

Card stock

ACID-FREE
Acid is used in paper manufacturing to break apart the wood fibers and the lignin that holds them together. If acid remains in the materials used for photo albums, the acid can react chemically with photographs and cause their deterioration. Acid-free products have a pH factor of 7.0 or above. It's imperative that all materials (glue, pens, paper, etc.) used in memory albums or scrapbooks be acid-free.

ACID MIGRATION
Acid migration is the transfer of acidity from one item to another through physical contact or acidic vapors. If a newspaper clipping is put into an album, the area it touches will eventually turn yellow or brown. A deacidification pH factor spray can be used on acidic papers, or they can be colorcopied onto acid-free papers.

ADHESIVE
Scrapbooking adhesives include a glue stick, double-stick tape, spray adhesive, thick white crafts glue, mounting tabs, and other products. Read the labels to determine the best adhesive for the intended use.

ARCHIVAL QUALITY
"Archival quality" is a term used to indicate materials that have undergone laboratory analysis to determine that their acidic and buffered content is within safe levels.

BORDERS
Borders are precut strips of patterned or solid paper used to add accent strips to a scrapbook page.

BUFFERED PAPER
During manufacture, a buffering agent, such as calcium carbonate or magnesium bicarbonate, can be added to paper to neutralize acid contaminant. Such papers have a pH of 8.5.

CARD STOCK
Often used for the base or background, card stock is a heavy paper with a smooth surface.

CORNER ROUNDER
Used like a paper punch, this tool rounds the corners of a photograph or paper.

CRAFTS KNIFE
Commonly known as an X-Acto knife, this tool has a small blade for cutting paper and other materials.

CROPPING
Cutting or trimming a photo to keep only the most important parts of the image is called cropping.

DECORATIVE-EDGE SCISSORS
Available in a wide assortment of cutting blades, these scissors cut paper and other thin materials with wavy, scalloped, zigzagged, or other decorative edges.

DIE CUT
This is a paper cutout in which the background is cut away. Die cuts come in hundreds of shapes and sizes.

GLOSSY
A smooth, shiny appearance or finish is referred to as glossy.

GLUE STICK
A glue stick is a solid stick-type glue that is applied by rubbing.

JOURNALING
Journaling refers to text on a scrapbook page that provides details about the photographs. Journaling can be done in your own handwriting, with adhesive letters, rub-ons, stencils, or it can be computer generated.

Corner rounder

Paper punch

Decorative-edge scissors

Die cuts

Stabilo pencil for marking backs of photos

Scrapbooking Glossary (continued)

Book of precut mat papers

LIGNIN
Lignin is the material that holds wood fibers together as a tree grows. If lignin remains in the final paper (as with newsprint), it will become yellow and brittle over time. Most paper other than newsprint is lignin-free.

MAT
Mats are varying weights of paper used to frame photographs using single or multiple layers.

MATTE
A dull surface or finish, not shiny or glossy, is considered matte.

OPAQUE
Colors that are dense and cannot be seen through are opaque.

PAPER CUTTER
A paper-cutting tool with a surface for holding the paper and a sharp blade that cuts the paper in a straight line.

PAPER PUNCH
Available in many different shapes, this handheld tool punches out circles, hearts, diamonds, and other shapes in stencil form.

Paper cutter

PH FACTOR
The pH factor refers to the acidity of a paper. The pH scale, a standard for measurement of acidity and alkalinity, runs from 0 to 14, each number representing a tenfold increase; neutral is 7. Acid-free products have a pH factor of 7 or above. Special pH tester pens are available to determine the acidity or alkalinity of products.

PHOTO-SAFE
Photo-safe is a term similar to "archival quality" but more specific to materials used with photographs. Acid-free is the determining factor for a product to be labeled photo-safe.

PROTECTIVE SLEEVES

Made of plastic to slip over a finished album page, sleeves can be side-loading or top-loading and fit 8½×11 or 12-inch-square pages. Choose only acid-free sleeves. Polypropylene (vinyl), commonly available for office use, is not archival quality and should not be included in albums.

RUBBER STAMPING

Designs are etched into a rubber mat that is applied to a wood block. This rubber design is stamped onto an ink pad to transfer the design to paper or other surfaces.

SCRAPBOOKING PAPERS

Scrapbooking papers are usually 12-inch squares or 8½×11-inch rectangles. These include solids, patterns, textures, and vellum.

SEPIA

This is a brown tone, usually associated with photographs, that has a warm, antique look.

STENCIL

Made from heavy paper or plastic, a stencil is laid flat on a surface, and paint or other medium is applied through the openings of the design to transfer it.

STICKERS

Available in plastic, paper, vinyl, fabric, and other materials, stickers can be peeled from a backing paper and pressed into place.

TRACING PAPER

A sheer sheet of paper that can be seen through, it is usually used to trace a pattern.

VELLUM

Available in white, colors, and patterns, this translucent paper has a frosted appearance.

Stickers

Stencil

Preserving Your Keepsakes

Photos are the heart of most scrapbooks, but remember other keepsakes. Collect everything! Save small items that relate to your theme, such as old letters, awards, certificates, ribbons, calling cards, a lock of hair, menus, place mats, brochures, business cards, newspaper and magazine articles, programs, announcements, matchbooks, and food wrappers. These items add interest to the pages. Even objects from nature make interesting mementos. Use a pH tester pen to determine the acidity or alkalinity of such items.

Because all of the elements in your album should be acid-free, it makes sense to store your supplies in archival-quality boxes and envelopes, which are available at most stores that carry scrapbook, photography, or stationery supplies.

You can protect scrapbook pages by photocopying items or by placing them in a clear, self-adhesive, acid-free memorabilia pocket available in several sizes with scrapbooking supplies.

Heirlooms, such as a brooch, pocket watch, or even a large quilt, are keepsakes worth preserving. To enjoy these items, photograph or copy them to include them in your heirloom scrapbook.

Include Precious Photographs

Preserve precious memories for future generations by including photographs that honor people, places, pets, or other noteworthy things in life. The first rule in sorting through photographs is to part with poor exposures. Those that are too dark, too light, out of focus, or meaningless should be discarded. Use only the best photographs for your scrapbook pages.

Sort photographs to relate to one another or to an album theme. You can affix the original photos in your album; however, if you want to save them for other purposes, photocopy the originals on a color photocopier.

If you have a collection of slides or reel-to-reel 8mm films, these can be converted to photographs at a relatively low cost at a photography supply shop or photo studio.

Identify as many people in your photos as possible, and add specific places and dates whenever possible. Ask older family members for help, and take your photos to family reunions and get-togethers for help in identification.

Handling Older Photographs

Be sure to wash your hands before handling your old photos. Dirt and oils from skin are damaging to photos and photo negatives.

A photo that has yellowed, become brittle, or been affixed with tape should be moved to a safer environment. However, you may want to copy the photo before moving it or have it professionally photographed in its current site.

Either use your heirloom photos in your album or make color photocopies of them. To capture all the shading of black-and-white or sepia-toned photos, make color photocopies of them, rather than making black-and-white photocopies. If you decide to use the original photos, consider securing them to the scrapbook pages with photo corners instead of permanently adhering them.

learn the basics

Good photography, composition, and journaling are key to successful scrapbook pages. Use the following information, tips, and techniques to master these basics. Discover what makes (or breaks) a dynamic photo. Uncover the secrets of composition without having to take a college course. Find out why journaling is so important and how to get the look and the words to complete your pages. These hints are from professionals in the fields of photography, design, and scrapbooking—so rest assured you're bound to learn something new to preserve your memories like never before.

Photography Tips and Ideas

{ABOVE} Avoid capturing too much background or extraneous items in photos. This photo lacks a focus and loses its impact because the subject is too far away. To correct this problem, zoom in on your subject. Unless the background has significant meaning, crop it out.

{ABOVE} This photo was taken with the sun behind the photographer's back. Because the light is shining directly into the boy's face, it causes him to squint. This type of lighting also casts vivid shadows, causing the loss of facial definition.

{ABOVE} With the light source coming from the side, this photo is somewhat better because some of the squinting is eliminated. However, the light angle creates unwanted shadows and the high camera angle doesn't allow the photo to capture the great expression on the boy's face.

{LEFT} With the sun at the boy's back, squinting is eliminated; however, the boy becomes a dark silhouette and the foreground details are lost. {RIGHT} This photo was taken on a sunny day in a shaded area. The sunlight is filtered through the trees, eliminating the boy's need to squint. Taken straight on, the boy's eyes look directly at the camera, and a pleasing smile is captured.

Photography Secrets from the Professionals

Great photographs make great scrapbooks. Carry your camera everywhere and keep these simple guidelines in mind whenever you want to capture a memory:

❧ BE GENEROUS WITH FILM. Opportunities will present themselves just once, and the price of film is minor when compared to the cost of a vacation or a once-in-a-lifetime experience.

❧ CAPTURE THE MOMENT. The best shots are unposed and capture the personalities of the subjects. Blurred movements rarely occur with today's super-fast films.

❧ RECORD THE MOMENT. Keep a small notebook with you so you can write down names, places, dates, and any other pertinent information about the people and the places you photograph.

❧ STAY CLOSE TO THE SCENE. Try to position the camera no more than 8 feet from the subject.

❧ TWO IS BETTER THAN ONE. Take one shot of the people, and then take a second shot of the background in order to set the mood.

❧ THROW SOME LIGHT ON IT. Early morning and late afternoon on a sunny day are ideal times for taking pictures; bright noonday sun creates harsh shadows and makes people squint their eyes. Gray days produce grainy photos.

❧ FOCUS, FOCUS, FOCUS. Most cameras will focus automatically. If you can adjust yours, be sure to adjust it as necessary before snapping the picture. Also, focus on what you are doing. If a toddler is tugging on your pant leg, it may be best to wait a minute before taking a photograph.

❧ BE MINDFUL OF THE BACKGROUND. When taking photographs of people or animals, check out the background. Make sure it won't overpower the subject. Sometimes just shifting your position will make for a more powerful photograph.

❧ CREATE AN EYE-CATCHING COMPOSITION. Rather than place your subject directly in the center of the photo, adjust your frame so the subject is about one-third of the way from the edge. The same rule applies when shooting a still life or landscape.

❧ BE CONSISTENT WITH FILM DEVELOPING. Whether you prefer glossy, matte, or something in between, keeping the finish consistent will give your scrapbook a planned, neat appearance.

❧ BRING OUT THE VERY BEST IN YOUR PICTURES. The next time you drop off film for developing, look for a self-serve kiosk that lets you make new prints and enlargements right from your pictures in just minutes. This tool also enables you to zoom, crop, adjust color, reduce red eye, and even to make sepia or black-and-white prints. Just bring in an existing print or one on a digital camera storage card, CD, or disk. Follow the on-screen directions and you're off and running!

❧ CROP WITH CARE. You've heard it before; measure twice, cut once. This rule holds true when it comes to cropping photographs. Make sure they are marked clearly before trimming.

Page Composition Tips and Ideas

This assortment of six layout variations uses the same group of beautiful floral photographs. Although there are many possibilities, these layouts teach basic design principles and can be adapted to suit your personal photographs, no matter what the subject.

Note: These layouts display good principles of simple photo arrangement. Embellishments and extensive journaling are excluded in order to focus solely on photo arrangements.

When creating a page, begin with your photos. They are the most important element on the page. Your page will result in a much more pleasing design if you begin with the photos and then decide on the embellishments. If you start with a background paper or other design element and try to work the photos into it, the layout may look disconnected or the photos will lack importance. Remember that the focus should be the photos or other display items. Use embellishments to enhance rather than overpower photos.

As you look at these pages and understand how they were put together, visualize your own photos in the arrangements.

{#1} This layout is formal, simple, clean, and symmetrical. The focus is equal on all the photos. Each photo is cropped to the same size as well as photographed similarly, all close up and with the same perspective. The perfectly centered headline does not overpower or detract from the photos. If more journaling is desired, the headline box could be enlarged and the journaling positioned under the headline, keeping the box centered. Imagine this layout with your favorite things, four favorite people, or one person close-up with four different expressions. Borders could be added if desired.

{#2} This symmetrical layout works for many subjects as well. The main focus here is the dramatic vertical photo in the center. The remaining six are secondary. You can use this same principle with a different number of photos, more or fewer, keeping an equal number on both sides to maintain a symmetrical appearance. The small headline allows the striking photo in the center to take precedence. Extra journaling could be added under the headline or under each photo, small and centered. Imagine this design used for your vacation photos, with a dramatic vertical landscape in the center surrounded by other smaller vacation photos.

headline without other journaling. If you wish, small centered journaling could be placed under the oval for a formal elegant look, or if your topic is more whimsical, the journaling could be done along the curves of the silhouettes or oval.

{#3} This arrangement works great for these floral photos. The photo on the left side worked well for this layout, allowing it to be separated into two sections, one above and one below the headline. Examine your photos to see if they would work for this technique. It helps if the upper portion of the photo includes the main focus and the lower section is secondary. Depending on the photo, you can simply cut it apart horizontally or remove the center section where the headline is inserted.

This layout is deliberately divided with the left side occupying slightly more than a third of the page. Each of the smaller photos is the same size and photographed from a similar vantage point.

{#4} This dramatic layout can easily be adapted to many photo subjects. The simpleness, created by few elements, boldness, and open space, make this a perfect layout for a treasured photo. The oval draws attention and highlights a special portrait. The smaller silhouetted shapes, going off the page from the lower left and upper right, lead directly into the main photo. The idea here is to boldly feature this oval photo. The few photos and open space allow for a decorative, elegant background treatment. An oval mat, double oval mat, or other decoration could be appropriate for this. Also notice on this oval floral photo that there are two spots where it works well to cut out elements beyond the oval. This is a nice layout to use a

{#5} This symmetrical formal layout emphasizes a special photo, such as the butterfly. The similar photos in the top row are cropped the same size and have equal space between, above, and on the sides. Plenty of open space around the oval gives it a clean and elegant look. The bold headline along the bottom is large enough to line up with the photos along the top of the page. If you chose to add journaling to this layout, small lines could be

continued on page 22

Page Composition Tips and Ideas (continued)

written under each photo. To maintain a cleaner look, journaling could be placed at the bottom and centered under the headline.

This layout works well to feature a family portrait in the large oval and the smaller boxes for individual closeup portraits. Use any number of photos across the top. Keep them equal size and with equal space between to maintain the symmetry. If you mount photos on border paper, maintain consistency.

Depending on your photo subject, you could do several things. The four photos across the top could each be the same width. They also could be all the same color mat or each one could be different, depending on the nature of your photos. The large oval mat could be consistent with the small ones or it could draw more attention by the addition of embellishments.

{#6} This informal layout suits a variety of subjects. Six photos and horizontal, vertical, diamond, and tilted rectangle shapes energize this layout. This type of layout works especially well for photos with action. The dominant photos take precedence over the small headline tucked in the corner.

When photos break into other photos as they do here, separate them with a narrow margin. The small diamond-cropped photo stands out placed over the enlarged vertical photo. This layout could also work well with several bold short journaling spots instead of a single headline. The journaling for this layout could be written sideways and at angles along photo edges. It could also be overlapped onto photos.

Organizing Your Layout

Photos are often taken of a particular subject that is loved. Then we find ourselves in the scrapbook store purchasing an overwhelming selection of everything on that subject from papers to stickers. It can be hard to limit the use of materials when there is so much to choose from, such as on the top spread on the page, *opposite*.

The two spreads, *opposite*, show the differences between an overly cluttered composition (at the *top*) and a slightly simpler one (*bottom*). The top version includes too many busy borders, the placement of photos is chaotic, silhouettes are not cropped well, and there is no focus. Even though the bottom example includes one more photo. it is much more organized. The cluttered version has too much in it, and tends to overwhelm and confuse. The second example is neat, clearly headlined, and interesting. You can do several things to clean up the clutter when you have many photos and embellishments.

Version #1: too cluttered

Version #2: full, yet organized

BACKGROUND—The background used in the top example is an appropriate paper for the subject with its nostalgic appeal. It has a border on one page and a coordinating pattern on the opposite page. To simplify it, silver and gray solid papers were chosen. BORDERS—Version #1 has three types of borders appropriate for the subject, but they are too distracting. Version #2 has simple narrow black lines that frame and neatly define the photo edges. ADDED ART ELEMENTS—Version #1 has dice, car stickers, art pieces that contain journaling, and more, all appropriate but not needed when accompanied by good photos that duplicate what they represent. Simple journaling is all that is needed on Version #2. CROP THE PHOTOS—Crop out all unnecessary background from the photos to focus on the topic. Exclude buildings, grass, streets, crowd backgrounds —anything that does not add interest to the photos. USE SILHOUETTES WISELY— Neatness is important. Notice the differences in the green and orange flamed truck in the upper right corner. The neatly trimmed car on Version #2 is much more visible. The silhouettes are overused in Version #1 while Version #2 has one main silhouette with several smaller ones neatly arranged.

ORGANIZE YOUR LAYOUT— Version #1 has many elements placed chaotically with most of the main photos the same size. The interesting car parts are scattered around the layout, photos are arranged at angles that make it difficult to know where to look first, and the tiny headline gets lost. To clean it up, the photos were organized into three main blocks. The interesting closeups of car pieces were neatly trimmed and framed close together. Your eye is easily drawn to the bold black and red headline that moves you from left to right and brings you to the main photo. The simple journaling quickly explains the story. The main photo is considerably larger and a focal point. If you are using many photos, the layout is easier to look at without photos angling. Version #2 uses the line of cars on top and the main car to move you in one direction rather than many directions.

Design Secrets from the Professionals

There are a few tricks to designing a scrapbook page. And it's amazing the little changes that affect the layout and transform a not-so-good design into one that is spectacular. Here are some tips to help you decide where to place elements on a page:

❧ Do a thumbnail sketch. On a piece of paper, draw the elements you want to include on a page. Revise the sketch until it is pleasing. Before adhering the real pieces in place, position everything so you are sure you like the placement. Arrange the elements so the eye travels from the top left corner to the bottom right of a page or spread.

❧ Create an interesting composition by placing photos of different shapes and sizes together on the page. Back some photos with colored papers cut out with decorative-edge scissors. Leave others unframed.

Using too many or too few photos will not give your page the impact it deserves.

❧ Crop photos for interest. If necessary, enlarge the photo and then crop the image. To help decide the crop, place a template or precut mat on top of the photo before cutting it.

❧ Don't use poor exposures. Blurry, dark, or other bad photographs will ruin a good scrapbook page.

❧ Choose complementary elements. Avoid papers that are too busy or bright so they don't overpower scrapbook items.

Journaling Tips and Ideas

Your scrapbook page won't be complete until you tell the story behind the photos. Add names, dates, words, or phrases, perhaps written on a stamped scroll or banner, to identify people and places and to help tell your story. Use acid-free pens and markers, available in a variety of colors, to handwrite the information. Or purchase rubber stamp alphabets in a style to suit your theme.

Recollections may seem trivial at the time—the weather, what you ate, a travel situation, something funny that happened—but these details will prove fascinating to those who read your scrapbook pages years from now.

Make journaling a family affair. Ask your spouse and your children about their favorite remembrances of holidays, vacations, birthdays, and family traditions, then record them. Identify as many people in your photos as possible, and add specific places and dates whenever possible. Ask older family members for help.

Your heritage album will be easier to read when you title the pages (or sections). It's easily done with a family member's name written in a calligraphy pen and framed like the photos.

When recording information in your family album, use your own handwriting. The warmth of penned notes and labels will give your album a personal touch that can't be generated with computer type.

Words That Speak Volumes

Headline and Journaling Ideas to Complete Your Scrapbook Pages

ANNIVERSARY
Celebrating "I Do" All
    Over Again
Time Flies When You're
    Having Fun
Silver (or Gold) Day
Memories
Two Became One

BABIES
Our Heaven-Sent Angel
He's (or She's) Precious in
    His Sight
Growing Up
Oh So Big!
Our Little Angel
Our Child, Our Gift
If We Could Only Keep
    Them Small

BIRTHDAY
What a Happy Occasion!
Look Who's Two
    (or three, or 40!)
Happy Birthday, Dear
    (fill in name)
Waaaay Over The Hill!
Oh Happy Day!
I Can Have My Cake and
    Eat It Too!
Happy Birthday to Me!

CHRISTMAS
Fa, La, La, La, La!
'Tis the Season!
Merry, Merry Christmas!
Season's Greetings
A Merry Little Christmas!

FAMILY
Happiness Is When
    Families Gather
I Love My Family
Family Times are the
    Best of Times
Families Are a Gift

FRIENDSHIP
Girls Just Wanna Have Fun
Friendship is a Gift
Thanks for Being My Friend
Friends Make the World
    Go Around
Friends Are the Sunshine
    of a Day

HALLOWEEN
A Frightfully Fun Night
Our Terror-ific Party

HANUKKAH
Happy Hanukkah
Lighting the Menorah

KIDS
All About ME
I Did It ALL BY MYSELF
Kids Do the Darndest Things

THANKSGIVING
It's Gobble, Gobble Time!
We Are So Thankful
Together Again!
When the Family Gathers...

TRAVEL
What a Great Time!
And We're Going
    Again...WHEN?!
A Vacation to Remember
An Unforgettable Visit
WOW! What a Vacation!
I'll Never Forget When We
    Went to (fill in location)

WEDDING
With This Ring I Thee Wed
Me and You...YAHOO!
Unforgettable
My Endless Love
I'd Do It All Over Again
No Regrets
What a Day!
Perfectly Blissful
My Love, My Friend
We Finally Tied the Knot!

OUR **KIDS**

Dance

Morgan started dance class in the Fall of 2001. She loved it from the very first day. Her recital is on June 15th, 2002.

and my new tap shoes!

my pretty new dance dress

2 x 2

ZACH

ANNA

Josh

from Grandma's piano to music major in college

2002

1986

it's all about the kids

They are funny, adorable, bashful, proud—yes, kids possess a million different characteristics, and each one is precious! Capture their expressions, talents, experiences, and passions on scrapbook pages that they will treasure for years to come. In this chapter devoted to kids, you'll learn great basic layouts along with fun new techniques and approaches to make the most of your keepsake photos. From cribs to baseball fields, dance recitals to Scouts, you'll be inspired to design pages devoted to your own special kids. After all, when it comes to the kids, you can never have too many scrapbook pages!

Our Kids

WHAT YOU'LL NEED
- 12-inch square of background card stock
- Coordinating 8½×11-inch papers
- ⅛-inch-wide embroidery ribbon and needle (available at fabric and crafts stores)
- Flat buttons
- Thick white crafts glue
- Computer and printer
- Adhesive
- Photos

Surround your favorite kids with blooms using three easy stitches. Before stitching, mark (but do not cut) photo cutout areas. To make the flowers, use a sharp needle and ribbon to make a French knot (see diagrams, *below left*) for each flower center. Surround each center with five lazy daisy petals, grouping some flowers together and letting others stand alone.

Accentuate the photo openings with running stitches around the edges. After stitching, cut out the marked photo areas using a crafts knife.

Glue narrow strips of the accent paper to the outer corners and trim them even with the mat paper.

Create a vertical headline, print on the accent paper, and adhere it to the background. Glue small buttons at the tip of each letter and randomly on the photo mat paper. Let the glue dry.

Carry the yellow accent to the outer edge with narrow strips.

Use a crafts knife to cut out areas for photos.

Add buttons to dress up a plain computer font.

Use running stitches to border photo cutouts.

Use crafts glue to hold buttons in place.

FRENCH KNOT   LAZY DAISY   RUNNING STITCH

Combine lazy daisies and French knots to make dimensional flowers.

Annē Mae

WHAT YOU'LL NEED

- *Papers or photocopies of paper on pages 161 and 163*
- *8½×11-inch card stock*
- *Deep blue paper*
- *Copier or scanner*
- *Crafts knife; scissors*
- *Marking pen; adhesive; photo*

CREATE THIS PAGE USING OUR EXCLUSIVE PAPERS ON PAGES 161 AND 163.

Create this page for a photo of your heaven-sent little one and the papers on *pages 161 and 163.* Use the paper just as it is or reduce or enlarge the elements to suit your needs. To enlarge the background paper on *page 161* to 8½×11 inches, enlarge it 102 percent. The frame and journaling box are provided full size.

Photocopy and cut out each shape. Glue the background paper on card stock. Glue the photo and frame onto blue paper and then onto the background. Glue on the journal box. Add journaling.

On *page 163,* there is also alternate art to use or photocopy, including a journal box, strips of star paper, and star circles. The strips can be trimmed and used as a photo mat. To cover the corner seams, cut out four circles and glue one over each corner.

Use the papers on pages 161 and 163 to create your page.

Select a photo with the baby's eyes looking up toward the angels.

Separate the painterly papers by mounting the top mat on solid blue.

Choose a banner from page 163 to record pertinent information.

All-American Athlete

WHAT YOU'LL NEED
- *12-inch square of sports-related paper*
- *Four 12-inch squares of paper*
- *Two 8½×11-inch pieces of thin corkboard*
- *Photo mat*
- *Sports appliqués (available in fabric and discount stores)*
- *Star stickers*
- *Paper cutter or crafts knife*
- *Computer and printer*
- *Newspaper clippings*
- *Adhesive*
- *Photos*

This high school senior will proudly recall his sports success on these outstanding scrapbook pages. Depending on the size of newspaper clippings, you can adjust the layout.

The left-hand page highlights a large clipping. Remember, you can enlarge items at a copy center on acid-free paper for added impact. Cover up unrelated articles appearing near the selected ones by placing cork-backed clippings over those areas.

The cork rectangle on the right-hand page acts as a bulletin board to attach photos, appliqués, and another newspaper article. To make the cork stand out from the handsome baseball paper background, mount it on red and blue papers or papers in school

Use a computer to print type.

Cover unrelated newspaper articles with pieces of cork.

Crop newspaper clippings to include in your pages.

Place star stickers across both pages to link them together.

Whatever activities your child excels in, he (or she) is a winner with this rewarding design.

colors. Use a purchased mat to frame a graduation photo. Leave wallet-size photos without mats. Other items you may wish to include on the bulletin board are awards, school buttons, friends' signatures, school logos, and photos of trophies.

To make the headline and name, type them on a computer and print them on neutral-color papers. Trim the papers to the desired sizes. Back the printed papers with black or colored papers, trim, and glue in place even with the edges of the background paper.

For page continuity, add a row of star stickers across the bottom of both pages and dot the "i" in the "All-American Athlete" headline with a star sticker.

For added detail, choose stitched appliqués related to the theme of the scrapbook page. Use crafts glue to adhere the appliqués to the background. Repeat appliqués such as the baseball bats and balls shown on the right-hand page for an artful touch.

Add journaling below the cork bulletin board if desired.

Include stitched appliqués to reinforce the sports theme.

Use cork for texture and to act as a bulletin board, ready for displaying.

Dot the "i" with a sticker.

Splish Splash

WHAT YOU'LL NEED

- *12-inch square of turquoise textured card stock*
- *Rubber ducky photo strip (Shotz Photo Papers)*
- *Yellow print alphabet stickers (The Paper Patch); white alphabet stickers (Chartpak)*
- *Print papers in turquoise and white, and yellow and white (The Paper Patch)*
- *Animated animal stickers (The Gifted Line)*
- *Paper cutter or crafts knife and metal ruler; adhesive; photo*

Babies and bath time are a winning combination for a good photograph. The purchased photo strip of the rubber ducks guides the color choices for paper and lettering.

To highlight the photo, glue the image on a piece of polka-dot paper and trim it ⅛ inch beyond the photo edge. Glue the layers to white and yellow floral paper and trim ½ inch beyond the edge. Note that the photo matting and lettering align. Continue the lettering below, using the top edge of the duck photo as a guide. Complete the message with small white capitalized letters.

Adhere a polka-dot paper strip from the photo mat to the right edge with a sticker line defining the lower edge. As a final touch, apply whimsical character stickers on the page to look as though they are sitting or walking along the papers.

Lettering aligns with left edge of photo for an organized appearance.

Two colors, turquoise and yellow, tie the page together.

These fun characters seem to make the baby in the photo smile.

A purchased photo strip emphasizes bath time even more clearly than the photo.

Emma and Grandma

WHAT YOU'LL NEED
- 8½×11-inch piece of ochre-color background card stock
- Lightweight tissue or rice paper, such as Mulberry paper (PrintWorks) in lavender, tan, and green
- Papers to frame the photo
- Papers for flowers, such as lavender, peach, yellow, and gold
- Paper cutter
- Spray adhesive (Elmer's)
- Scallop-edge decorative scissors and straight scissors
- Paper punch: marking pen
- Adhesive: photo

You may have a special photo, such as this autumn scene, that inspires you to create a handmade background. To choose the best papers, take the photo with you to the store. The lavender sky and the tan and green foliage are made from tissue-like papers. To achieve this look, glue the lavender tissue sky on the top portion of the ochre-color background paper. Cut corn and leaves from tan and green paper strips and glue them in place.

To make paper flowers, cut circles from colored paper using scallop-edge scissors. Cut tiny slits around the edges with straight scissors. Punch flower centers from gold paper. Shape the flowers and glue them in place.

Use a marking pen to add journaling to a matted paper piece.

Contrasting paper mats separate the photo from the background.

Lightweight tissue-like paper simulates the fall foliage in the photo.

Colors in the photo are replicated on the scrapbook page.

Cut circles with scallop-edge scissors and fringe them to make small blooms.

Glue on paper flowers last to overlap the photo and journaling.

Emma and Grandma -fall of '94

Student Driver

WHAT YOU'LL NEED
- *Two 8 ½×11-inch pieces of blue background card stock*
- *Black paper*
- *Grass-pattern paper (Provo Craft)*
- *Solid gray, yellow, brown, and white papers*
- *Crafts knife*
- *Black marking pen*
- *Adhesive*
- *Photos*

To create photos to personalize scrapbook pages, take your camera to unexpected places and events, such as Driver's Education class.

Take photos to tell a story. Rather than searching for perfect art elements, photograph your own embellishments, such as road signs

A close-up photograph of a vehicle sticker is used for the headline.

Use a permanent black marking pen to add journaling to photos.

Cut conversation bubbles and arrow shapes from white paper to use as backgrounds for personalized journaling.

Simple narrow black borders work well in this busy format.

Here's a topic every teen will want to remember, and many parents may want to forget! This driver's education class is whimsically displayed with fun captions and oodles of real-road details.

and a student driver sign to use for the headline. This photo was taken from the side of the vehicle and trimmed.

To re-create these pages, layer the elements on 8½×11-inch blue background papers. Cut grass paper for the lower portion, curved strips of gray paper, and a dotted yellow line for the road. Cut varying lengths of signposts from brown paper.

Use a black marking pen to add journaling in the white shapes cut from white paper.

A silhouetted truck photo, tilted, with white marking pen lines, creates animation.

Trim road sign photos and adhere to brown paper posts.

Peas in a Pod

WHAT YOU'LL NEED

- *Papers or photocopies of papers on pages 165–173*
- *12-inch square of card stock*
- *Scissors; crafts knife*
- *Colored pencils*
- *Green marking pen*
- *Adhesive*
- *Photos*

CREATE
THIS PAGE
USING OUR
EXCLUSIVE PAPERS
ON PAGES
165–173.

Here is a solution to a problem many of us have when taking photos of our little ones. These siblings posed for a photo and numerous shots were taken. When the film was developed, there wasn't one good photo of all three kids. To make a super scrapbook page, three different photos were enlarged and cropped to capture each child's best expression.

The background papers, borders, and cutouts are on *pages 165–173.* For a 12-inch-square page, enlarge the pea paper (*page 165*), plaid paper (*page 167*), and vine borders (*page 169*) at 111 percent on a photocopier. Cut a 6-inch-wide vertical section from the pea paper and adhere to the center of the page. Cut two 1¾-inch-wide strips from plaid paper. Adhere to background paper at the outer edges. Cut out the vine strips and adhere 1½ inches from the sides, covering the edges of the pea and plaid papers.

Cut out the desired headline from *page 173,* pea pod from *page 171,* and journal box and circle from *page 169.* Adhere to the page in that order. On *pages 169–173* there are alternate pieces of art to photocopy, including journal boxes, a pea pod, and a headline.

To make the photos appear as one, color around the edges with colored pencil, the same color or darker.

Enlarge the photos if necessary and carefully crop around the faces.

Copy and trim the art elements from pages 165-173.

Layer papers starting with the pea-dotted background, then layer the plaid and vine borders, headline banner, pea pod, journaling box, and decorative circle.

Close-up shots of kids' faces are highlighted in this sweet design. While there are three "peas" in this pod, you can adapt the layout to include the little angels in your garden.

Birthday Bash

WHAT YOU'LL NEED

- *12-inch squares of card stock in blue, green, and goldenrod*
- *Frames and die cuts (Cock-a-doodle)*
- *Balloon buttons (Jesse James Button Co.)*
- *Fibers (Making Memories)*
- *Foam squares (Therm-o-Web)*
- *Scissors*
- *Adhesive*
- *Photos*

Broad horizontal stripes create a fun, yet organized background for this birthday tribute. Choose the background papers, die cut, and frames at the same time to coordinate the colors.

Adhere birthday die cuts for a festive "happy birthday" touch. Glue button balloons on the page to fill in. To make the balloons stand out on the page, mount them on small foam squares. Tie long threads to the balloons in groups of two or three.

Trim the headline lettering, leaving a narrow white border beyond the words to separate it from the colored background.

Place the journaling neatly in a mat to complete the spread.

Trim purchased lettering to make the headline pop from the background.

Angle photos in different directions to balance the left and right pages.

Use balloon buttons mounted on foam squares for dimension.

Include a variety of fibers to add color to each page.

Cut apart die cuts to make three candles for the cupcake.

Use a computer font for journaling.

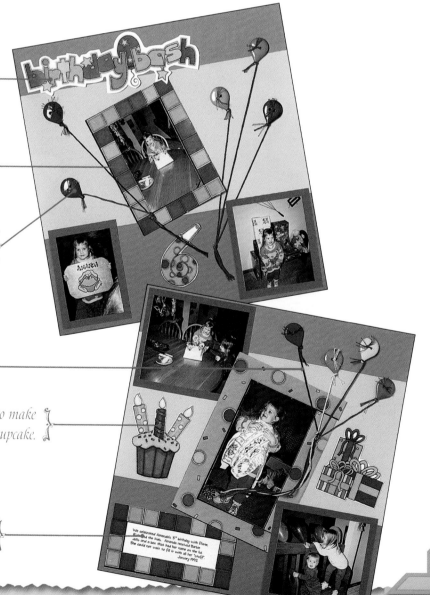

Swing Choir

WHAT YOU'LL NEED

- *12-inch square of striped card stock*
- *12-inch square of coordinating check paper*
- *Clear gel glue (Suzy's)*
- *Fine blue glitter (The Art Institute)*
- *Marking pen*
- *Scissors*
- *Adhesive*
- *Photos*

Two-tone pink papers create a soft background for this special occasion. To add weight to the bottom, a coordinating paper was cut in half and glued horizontally across the page.

The sparkle of these dancers' attire is captured in the glistening headline. To get the look, write the heading on the background paper using gel glue. While the glue is wet, sprinkle with glitter. Let the glue dry. Shake off extra glitter.

Crop the photos and choose one to silhouette. Tuck these figures behind a rectangular photo to anchor them on the page.

To make the musical staff, use a marking pen to draw freehand wavy lines. Add musical notes with glue and glitter. Write in photo captions and this page is done quicker than you can say "encore!"

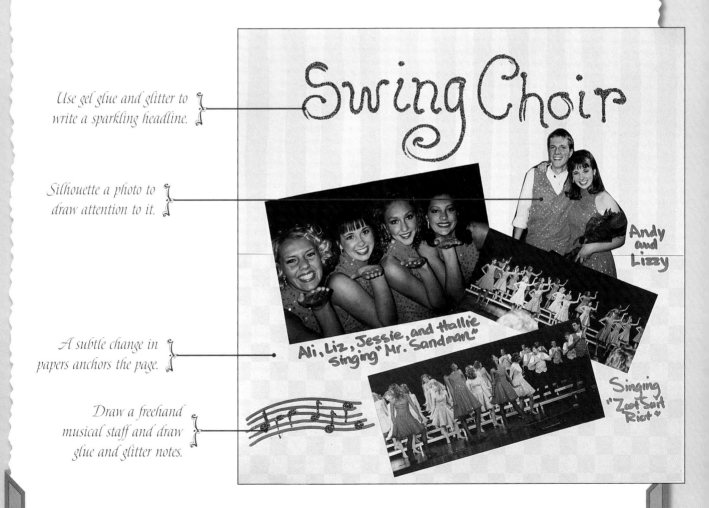

Use gel glue and glitter to write a sparkling headline.

Silhouette a photo to draw attention to it.

A subtle change in papers anchors the page.

Draw a freehand musical staff and draw glue and glitter notes.

Dance

WHAT YOU'LL NEED

- *Tracing paper and pencil*
- *Scissors*
- *Two 12-inch squares of background paper (Sweetwater)*
- *12-inch square of coordinating patterned paper (Sweetwater)*
- *Two 12-inch square pieces of card stock*
- *Coordinating paper scraps for shoes and photo mats (Sweetwater)*
- *Tape; transfer paper*
- *½-inch-wide ribbon and ⅛-inch-wide satin ribbon*
- *White paper*
- *Scallop-edge decorative scissors*
- *Fine-line black permanent marking pen*
- *Floral photo corners (Stickopotomus)*
- *Bouquet sticker (Stickopotomus)*
- *Adhesive; photos*

When you want to make two pages with a dance theme, this little number will do the trick. To make the tutu, cut the printed paper in half.

Fold the printed paper pieces back and forth to create pleats, making irregular folds. Crease the folds and tape across the top back to hold the pleats in place.

Enlarge the pattern, *page 42*, at 200 percent on a photocopier. Trace the patterns. Cut out the skirt, shoe, and leg patterns. Place the tutu pattern over the folded paper, align at the straight edges, trace, and cut out. Trace around the leg shapes on white paper and the shoe shapes on printed paper. Cut out the shapes.

Use scallop-edge scissors to cut a dainty border around photos.

Draw dotted lines to detail and define the shapes.

When a little ballerina is just learning the difference between a plié and first position, the costumes can be the most fun of all. This folded-paper tutu sets the stage for any collection of dance photos.

Use a glue stick to adhere the shoes to the feet. Glue a leg on each page. Glue a skirt half over each leg. Glue ½-inch-wide ribbon pieces along the top edge of each skirt piece. Tie a generous bow and glue to the ribbon on the right-hand side.

Glue a narrow piece of ribbon to each shoe heel and angle it over the ankle. Tie a ribbon bow for each lace and tack them in place using a floral corner over the center of each bow.

Make dotted lines around each shoe and the pages.

Cut two photos using an oval template. Silhouette a large photo, letting it extend off the right page. Adhere the oval photos to background papers and trim with decorative-edge scissors.

Add marking pen dots to each scallop. Overlay the ovals with floral stickers.

Use transfer paper to transfer the headline to the upper left corner. Draw dotted swirls, the headline, and journaling using a marking pen.

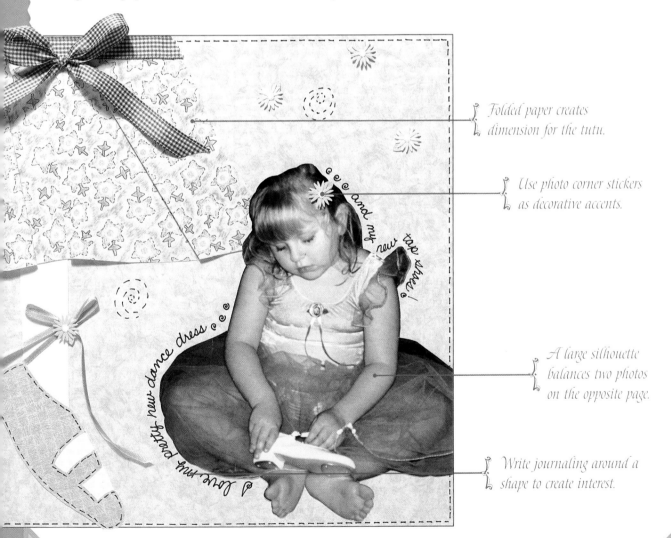

Folded paper creates dimension for the tutu.

Use photo corner stickers as decorative accents.

A large silhouette balances two photos on the opposite page.

Write journaling around a shape to create interest.

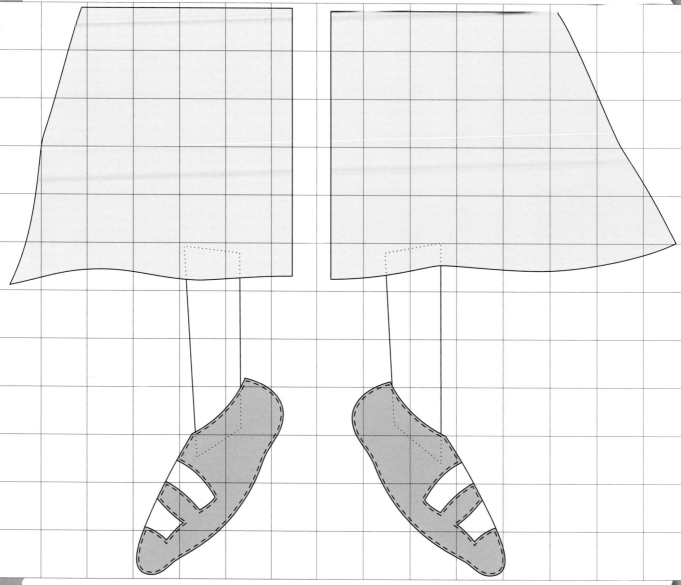

DANCER PATTERNS

1 SQUARE = 1 INCH

Dance

HEADLINE PATTERN

Baby Album

WHAT YOU'LL NEED

- 7¼×5½-inch pieces of white card stock
- Pink print paper (All My Memories)
- Green print paper (Frances Meyer)
- Yellow card stock
- Pink letters (Making Memories)
- Month by Month Stickers (SRM Press)
- Stickers (Colorbök and Stickopotomus)
- Small vellum poem sticker (Highsmith)
- Large vellum poem sticker (Once Upon A Scribble)
- Adhesive; photos

This adorable brag book will make any mom or grandma proud. Using only three decorative papers and ready-made stickers and other embellishments, you can create an entire booklet in just a few hours.

Study these pages and note how strips and blocks of the print papers trim each page. After the photos are cropped and backed, decorate the background space with stickers, fabric embellishments, journaling, colored paper pieces—whatever you wish to fill the space and complete the tiny pages.

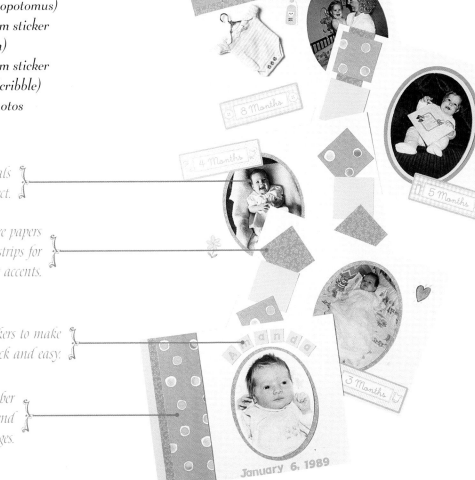

Crop photos in ovals to highlight the subject.

Cut decorative papers in squares and strips for page accents.

Use stickers to make journaling quick and easy.

Limit the number of papers to three to lend continuity to the pages.

Cub Scout Pride

WHAT YOU'LL NEED

- Two 12-inch squares of white scrapbook papers
- Cub Scout scarf
- Tape
- Papers in white, red, yellow-orange, and navy
- Scissors and pinking shears
- Crafts knife
- Star stickers in gold and red
- Red alphabet stickers
- Adhesive
- Photos and photocopy of certificate

When scouring the hundreds of beautiful papers for one that is just right, keep your mind open to other materials, such as this Cub Scout scarf.

To adhere the scarf to the full sheet of white paper, trim the raw edges of the scarf approximately ½ inch beyond the paper edge. Align the finished scarf edges with the paper edges, and fold the raw edges over the paper. Crease the folds, pressing if necessary. Glue the scarf to the right side of the paper. On the back side of the paper, tape the raw edges of the scarf in place. For the right-hand page, glue a remaining corner of the scarf diagonally on the page.

Use scarf scraps for bold accents.

Layer mats to pull the page colors together.

Use a fabric scarf to create a graphic background.

Whether coloring a pretty picture, getting good grades, or winning a contest, kids have hundreds of reasons to be proud. These pages, complete with ear-to-ear smiles, mark an occasion to commemorate.

Create the headline banner from a strip of white paper. Use a navy stripe from a scarf scrap at the top. Layer the banner on red paper, pinking the red edging. Adhere bold vertical lettering and official-looking metallic gold stars.

Layer paper mats for two of the photos and silhouette two photos. Because this award was for a cake design, a photo of the popcorn cake was enlarged on a color photocopier and silhouetted to draw attention to it.

If you include an award certificate, apply star stickers to carry out the stars on the headline banner.

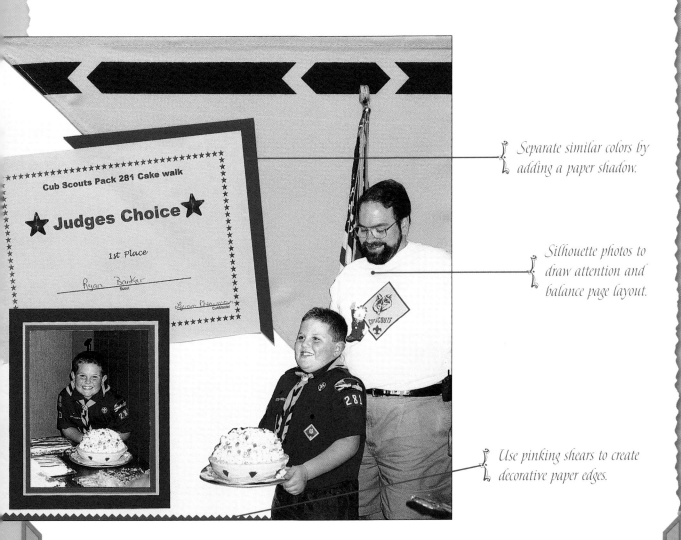

Separate similar colors by adding a paper shadow.

Silhouette photos to draw attention and balance page layout.

Use pinking shears to create decorative paper edges.

45

2x2—Twins Turn Two

WHAT YOU'LL NEED
- *Tracing paper and pencil*
- *Straight and decorative-edge scissors*
- *12-inch square of turquoise polka-dot paper (me & my BIG ideas)*
- *White card stock*
- *Colored papers in green, purple, orange, and yellow*
- *Yellow acrylic paint; paintbrush*
- *Yellow tube-style paint*
- *Striped paper; adhesive; photos*

While this page touts twins turning 2, the headline could be adapted to focus on one child's big day. For birthday headline options, get some ideas on *page 25*.

To make the cake photo mats and headline, enlarge the patterns, *below left*, 200 percent on a photocopier. Trace and cut out the shapes. Trace around the cake and number shapes on white card stock. Cut out the shapes. Cut out a white X.

Trace around the plate shape on colored paper. Cut it out and glue it on the white card-stock cake. Paint yellow frosting, leaving a white border. Let the paint dry. Dot tube paint around the frosting. Let it dry.

Use the patterns to cut candles from patterned paper and flames from solid paper. Use pinking shears to cut small paper accents.

CAKE, CANDLES, AND NUMBERS PATTERNS   1 SQUARE = 1 INCH

Paper strips cut with pinking shears add color and movement to the background.

Set the stage for a celebration with birthday cake photo mats.

Personalize the cake mats using a black marking pen.

Choose a background paper with a subtle confettilike design so as not to overpower the photos.

Record magical cake-eating moments to remember for many birthdays to come. While this page honors twins, you can adapt the headline and candle count to celebrate your birthday girl or boy.

Sand Volleyball

WHAT YOU'LL NEED

- 12-inch squares of grass print paper
- Sand print paper (Wubie Prints)
- Wire mesh (Scrap Yard)
- String
- Scissors
- Silver Diamond Dust paper (Paper Adventures)
- Self-sealing clear pocket (3L Memorabilia Pockets)
- Die-cut letters (Dayco)
- Volleyball stickers (All My Memories)
- Journaling volleyball (Little Extra)
- Adhesive
- Photos

Selecting the right papers can set the tone for the page. These grass and sand papers are good choices for a competitive game of sand volleyball.

Before applying the sand print paper on the grass paper background, tear the edges of two sheets to make similar-size squares and glue in place.

Crop the photos and glue them in place. Notice how some photos are behind or partially behind the netting. Place volleyball stickers on a couple of photos to appear as balls in motion.

Real wire mesh creates the appearance of a volleyball net.

A round die cut works perfectly for journaling.

Playing volleyball at the lake is always alot of fun. Dawn, Doug, & Michelle played with all the kids. They played for over 2 hours. Alex found other things to do in the sand!! Ozarks 2002

Create a winner of a page that highlights the sport of outdoor volleyball. Wire mesh creates an interesting net that spans across the sandy pages.

Stretch pieces of wire mesh across each page and tack them in place. Make the poles using silver diamond dust paper. Add pieces of string so the net appears tied to the poles.

To create the headline, trace around letters on sand print paper and cut out. For the letters S and V, adhere each inside a clear pocket, add a pinch of sand, and seal the pockets. Adhere a pocket in place on each page and complete the words using the remaining letters.

Add journaling to a volleyball die cut. Place a small strip of netting behind the circle and adhere both in place.

Use scraps of sand print paper to make the headline.

Place volleyball stickers strategically on photos to reinforce the theme.

Embellish the poles with string ties for a realistic look.

Abby

WHAT YOU'LL NEED
- 12-inch square of plaid background paper (Doodlebug)
- Green paper (Two Busy Moms)
- Tulip journal box and floral letters software (Creating Keepsakes)
- Scissors
- Adhesive
- Photos

Simplicity is the key to this endearing page. Four basic shapes (rectangles, triangles, squares, and a tulip) and two colors (pink and green) work together for a graphic presentation.

For the headline, print floral letters on white paper and trim the same width as the green paper strip. Trim at the top and bottom, leaving a border of green. Cut squares of pink plaid paper and turn on point. Adhere the squares to the green paper strip. For a longer name, overlap the points of the squares or choose smaller lettering. Contain the journaling in a flower shape to lend importance to the words.

If using similar photos, enlarge one so they seem to have been taken at different distances. Use a corner rounder to soften the photo edges. Center the larger photo below the two smaller shapes to balance the page design.

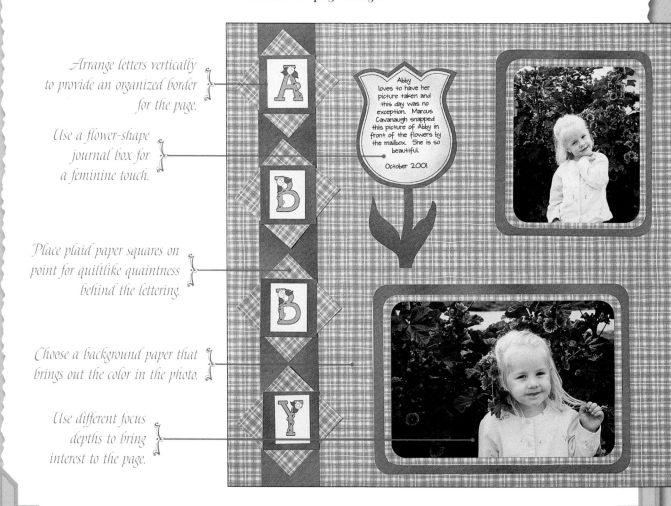

Arrange letters vertically to provide an organized border for the page.

Use a flower-shape journal box for a feminine touch.

Place plaid paper squares on point for quiltlike quaintness behind the lettering.

Choose a background paper that brings out the color in the photo.

Use different focus depths to bring interest to the page.

Abby loves to have her picture taken and this day was no exception. Marcus Cavanaugh snapped this picture of Abby in front of the flowers by the mailbox. She is so beautiful.

October 2001

Josh

WHAT YOU'LL NEED
- *8½×11-inch piece of black paper*
- *Paper cutter*
- *Silver paper*
- *Die cuts of musical elements*
- *Silver rub-on tint*
- *White opaque marker*
- *Adhesive*
- *Photos*

This quick-to-do page, simply named by the subject, is created with few materials. To create the treble clef and wavy lines in the background, use purchased die cuts. To achieve an embossed look, use the same color die cuts as the background paper (in this case, black). Highlight the die cuts by rubbing on silver tint to give them more definition without overpowering the page.

Mount each photo on silver paper and trim for narrow borders. To keep the photos as large as possible, extend them to the edge of the page.

Using the photos and staff lines as guides, add journaling and dates with a white marking pen.

Mat on silver for a classy frame on each photo.

Handwrite white journaling for a striking accent on black.

Overlap an older black and white photo with a current color photo.

Apply silver rub-on tint to cutouts to highlight.

Add dimension with music staff die cuts.

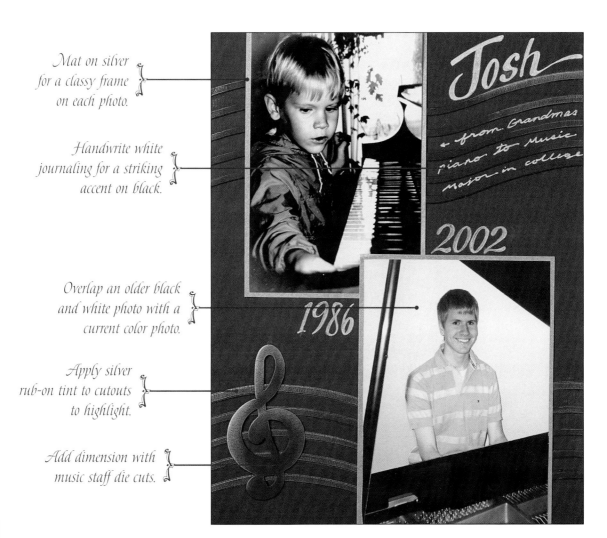

Happy Birthday

WHAT YOU'LL NEED

- *Tracing paper; pencil*
- *Two 12-inch squares of white background paper*
- *Balloon pattern paper (Paper Patch)*
- *Confetti paper (Paper Patch)*
- *Blue floral paper (Paper Patch)*
- *Goldenrod paper*
- *Chalk (Craf-T)*
- *Party hat die cut (Die Cuts with a View)*
- *Numeral punch (EK Success)*
- *Marking pen (Zig)*
- *Journal balloons (Creating Keepsakes)*
- *Scissors*
- *Double-stick tape*
- *Adhesive; photos*

When these pages are turned to, it's easy to see that a party is going on. The lively balloon and confetti papers set a festive mood. The center pop-up, looking like a slice of cake, is easily created from paper that is cut, folded, and mounted to the pages using double-stick tape. To make the pop-up, enlarge the patterns, *opposite*, at 200 percent on a photocopier. Trace around the pop-up pattern on confetti paper and the candles on contrasting paper. Cut out the shapes.

Create lettering on a computer, print it, and color it in using a marking pen. Adhere the lettered pieces to the candle backgrounds and apply to the base pop-up piece.

Silhouette photos to provide focus on the subject matter.

Blend colored chalk around the edges of the balloon shapes to soften the look.

With a center pop-up like those found on greeting cards, these scrapbook pages hold an unexpected birthday surprise.

Add journaling in balloon shapes of varying sizes. Soften the edges of the balloons with colored chalk.

Use solid-color photo inner mats to separate the busy outer mat and photos from the background, making them the focal points of the pages.

HAPPY BIRTHDAY PATTERNS

1 SQUARE = 1 INCH

Use two thicknesses of paper to support the pop-up center.

Secure the pop-up with tacky double-stick tape.

Alex made this poster all by himself and gave it to Abby. He was so proud of it we put it on the fireplace to show it off.

Alex digs in to one of the Barbie cupcakes.

Abby was thrilled to get her very own Tootsie Roll bank. She would always raid Jeffrey's tootsie rolls when she went to their house so they got her a "stash" of tootsie rolls. They were gone in a day!

Cut solid yellow inner mats to separate the photos from the busy outer mats and background paper.

Soccer

WHAT YOU'LL NEED
- Blue star pattern paper (Sandylion)
- Card stock in black and white
- Die cut letters (Dayco)
- Mini soccer stickers (SRM)
- Goal sticker (me & my BIG ideas)
- Adhesive
- Photos

When you have numerous people in photos, such as on a sports team, choose subtle backgrounds that do not overpower the photo. This blue-on-blue star paper adds soft texture to the background. (It also quietly states that you're a star!)

Mat the three photos with black so they pop on the page and use varying-size cropped photos for interest and to help the eye travel around the page.

Soccer accents, such as the headline, stickers, and journal shapes carry out the theme. Apply the "Goal!" sticker to white and trim it evenly beyond the sticker.

Angle the headline letters for a lighthearted look and apply soccer ball stickers to the letters.

Place soccer stickers on each letter to reinforce the theme.

Mount a vellum sticker on white card stock for emphasis.

Use black mats to separate photos from background.

Choose a subtle print that does not distract from the photos.

Place journaling in a soccer ball die cut.

During the first soccer game Alex was so excited he made two goals. One for our team and one for the other team!

Snow Fun

WHAT YOU'LL NEED

- Card stock in blue and white
- Stickers (All My Memories)
- White opaque marking pen (EK Success)
- Adhesive
- Photos

It's a visual relief in scrapbooks to vary the placements. This wintry collection of photos is placed around the headline that is centered on the page. Apply headline stickers to white paper and trim for added emphasis.

For the top and bottom borders, use stickers in a row placed horizontally on the page. When creating several scrapbook pages with the same theme, this element can be consistently used to lend continuity to the pages.

Crop some of the photos rectangular and some round to provide variety and to help balance the symmetry.

With a blue background dark enough to accommodate white journaling, use an opaque white pen for writing and drawing snowflakes on the page.

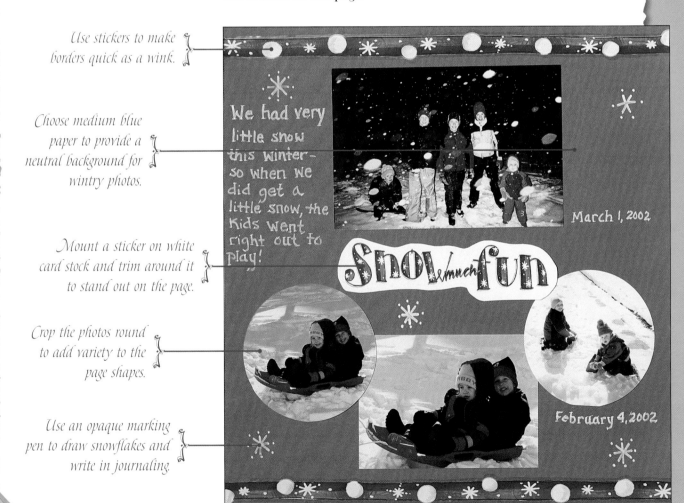

Use stickers to make borders quick as a wink.

Choose medium blue paper to provide a neutral background for wintry photos.

Mount a sticker on white card stock and trim around it to stand out on the page.

Crop the photos round to add variety to the page shapes.

Use an opaque marking pen to draw snowflakes and write in journaling.

We had very little snow this winter- so when we did get a little snow, the kids went right out to play!

March 1, 2002

Snow much fun

February 4, 2002

Marching Band

WHAT YOU'LL NEED
- Two 12-inch squares of white card stock
- Six accent papers in bright colors
- White paper
- Rainbow color rickrack
- Musical note stamp
- Gold stamp pad
- Scissors: circle cutter
- Paper cutter
- Stitched appliqué letters (available in the notion section of fabric and discount stores)
- Line stickers (Mrs. Grossman)
- Floral buttons
- Black fine-line marking pen
- Adhesive: photos

Everyone loves a parade, and this bright design captures all the fun of a neighborhood march.

To start this page, cut colored paper bands for the headline lettering and star, leaving approximately ½ inch around the appliqués on all sides. To make the M and B stand out, cut circles from contrasting paper. Glue the circles to the strips. Adhere the letters and glue the strips to the background, leaving space for the rickrack. Glue rickrack across both pages.

Crop the photos using round, rectangular, and silhouetted shapes. Close-up shots of the instruments add an important touch to the page.

Use stitched appliqués horizontally and vertically for a striking headline.

Place colored circles under letters to lead your eye.

Follow a mat shape with journaling to keep the page neat.

Use a musical note stamp to emphasize the band theme.

56

*An impromptu neighborhood parade is reason to
celebrate, and this marching-band display doesn't miss a beat.*

Mount the photos on white and colored papers and trim as
desired using as many mats as needed to separate the photos from
the background.

To create a horizon line for the silhouetted kids to stand on, glue
a colored piece of paper to the right-hand page. Press line stickers
along the edge for added detail.

Stamp music notes near some of the instruments, following the
cut paper edges as guides. Use crafts glue to glue buttons in place.
Let the glue dry.

Use a marking pen to add journaling, keeping the writing
organized by following the shapes of the photos.

*Glue rickrack across the
top of both pages to tie
them together.*

*Snip the shanks
from buttons and glue
the buttons in place
using crafts glue.*

*Repeat circular shapes
throughout the peppy layout.*

SPAIN

Katherine, left Alcazar Segovia Cathedral and Aquaduct

Sandcastles

Sanibel Island

Seagulls

Shells

THE BIG APPLE

New York, New York

DRIVING ALONG THE LONG ROAD TO GEYSER.

JEFF AND WILL LOOKING AT THE SHIFT OF THE CONTINENTAL PLATES.

RIDING THE ICELANDIC HORSES.

ICELAND

remembering life's favorite travels

Capture vacation experiences on film to reflect on the fun and relive the moments. Gather your favorite travel photos and get ready to organize them on scrapbook pages that burst with creativity. From building sandcastles along the shore to camel rides in the desert, from exploring beautiful Iceland to touring exciting attractions in America, this idea-packed chapter gives you a suitcase full of tips to make the most of your travel photos and mementos.

Morocco in June

WHAT YOU'LL NEED
- *Two 12-inch squares of tan background paper*
- *Sunburst yellow card stock*
- *Deckle-edge decorative scissors (Fiskars)*
- *Corner rounder (Creative Memories)*
- *Sunburst template (Frances Meyer)*
- *Lettering template*
- *Computer and printer*
- *Fiber (Making Memories)*
- *Yellow eyelets (Stamp Doctor)*
- *Eyelet tool; paper punch*
- *Light orange decorating chalks*
- *Alphabet template*
- *Thick white crafts glue*
- *Adhesive*
- *Photos*

Whether traveling abroad for an exotic vacation or to the neighbor's backyard for a quaint garden tea, be sure to take along your camera and plenty of film. If you are lucky, you'll end up with oodles of photos that will retell the story of the day for you and future generations.

When you have several quality photos to pack onto a spread, such as the eight Morocco photos shown *below*, simplicity can be the answer. Special touches, such as rounding the photo corners and matting them with colored paper, using large headlines, placing journaling in blocks, and tying fibers in knots, enlivens the page.

Knot fibers for a natural touch to your vacation spread.

Use one decorative-edge pair of scissors for continuity.

Our ferry ride brought us to the beautiful, the exciting, the fascinating...

Morocco

Our first stop in Morocco was camel riding.

Left – Megan Garrett
Below – Jen Strabbing

Capture the excitement of summertime vacations on film and show off your photo collection on well-organized pages. This sunny arrangement, packed with memories, is simple to achieve.

To create the center sunburst shape and headlines, use templates and yellow card stock. Shadow the sunburst rays with orange chalk. Cut the sunburst in half and apply each half to facing pages, aligning the straight edges.

Print journaling on yellow card stock with a computer font to highlight the main captions or thoughts. Trim the journaling into rectangles using the same decorative-edge scissors used to trim the photo mats.

Punch holes for eyelets. Affix an eyelet in each hole. To add a natural textural element, tie pairs of fiber pieces through the eyelets, slightly covering the edge of selected photos and at the page edges.

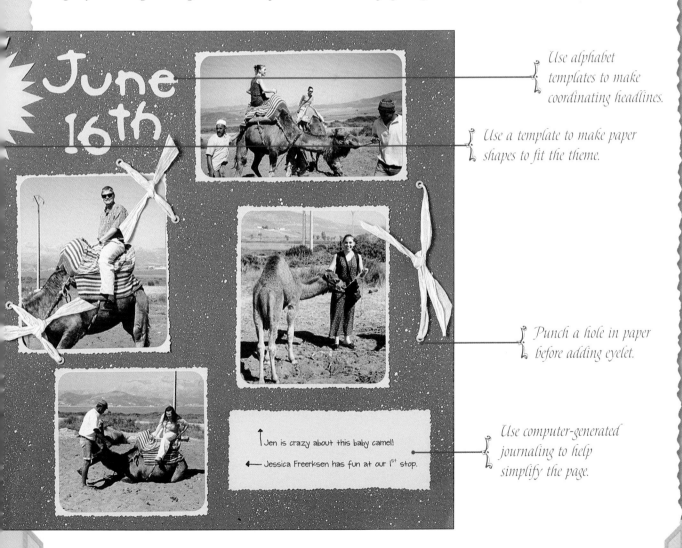

Use alphabet templates to make coordinating headlines.

Use a template to make paper shapes to fit the theme.

Punch a hole in paper before adding eyelet.

Use computer-generated journaling to help simplify the page.

June 16th

Jen is crazy about this baby camel!

Jessica Freerksen has fun at our 1st stop.

Spain

WHAT YOU'LL NEED
- 12-inch square of black background paper
- Paper that complements the headline photo
- Computer and printer
- Paper cutter
- Crafts knife
- Spray adhesive
- Adhesive
- Photos

A bonus to this stunning page is that it can be created with only two paper colors. To create a short headline, choose one of your photos, such as this landscape. If necessary, enlarge the photo to the size needed to span the size of the scrapbook page.

To make a pattern for the lettering, choose a bold chunky computer font. Print the word in reverse (mirror image or flipped horizontally). Using spray adhesive, adhere the photo to the back of the printed word. Cut out the letters.

Plan the journaling and photo arrangement before cropping the photos. After the sizes are determined, trim each photo, including any silhouetted areas. Cut paper that coordinates with the headline photo and use it to mat the photos.

Extend the letters to the top and side edges of the background paper.

Use bold type and a striking photo to create the headline.

Silhouette a snapshot of a person and glue it over a scenic photo.

Use a paper color that enhances the headline photo.

Use narrow borders and rectangular photos to simplify the design.

Iceland

WHAT YOU'LL NEED

- 12-inch square of background paper (The Paper Loft)
- Parchment, vellum, and other papers in shades of gray
- Computer and printer
- Crafts knife
- Adhesive
- Photos

Geometric shapes and shades of gray make an interesting combination for these travel photos of Iceland. These black and white photographs include a panoramic photo at the top with two close-up shots below. To re-create this look with colored photos, take the photos to a copy center and have them photocopied in black and white.

The background paper, designed in rectangular quadrants of color, sets the mood for this icy scene. To create the design beneath the headline, turn the papers on point and overlap the corners. Trim the pieces along the edge of the paper and glue them in place. Print a headline and photo captions to complete this quick-to-do page.

Use a panoramic shot to set the mood for a vacation spread.

Trim the caption for an arrow at one end.

Choose a geometric background to pull a graphic layout together.

Turn papers on point to make a design element.

Use a bold font in black to stand out on a gray-tone page.

DRIVING ALONG THE LONG ROAD TO GEYSER.

RIDING THE ICELANDIC HORSES.

JEFF AND WILL LOOKING AT THE SHIFT OF THE CONTINENTAL PLATES.

ICELAND

St. Michael's

WHAT YOU'LL NEED
- *Two 12-inch squares of background paper*
- *Paper cutter*
- *Neutral paper for photo mounting*
- *Computer and printer*
- *Black fine-line marking pen*
- *Adhesive*
- *Photos*

You may have a special place you want to remember always, such as this old church. Photographs of this historical church were taken after it was closed to regular services. If you have a place like this from your childhood, take the time now to photograph whatever you can, especially those things that have special meaning to you. Inquire with people associated with a building whether they can share related photos or experiences from the past. Historical photos often add an emotional touch to scrapbook pages.

This heavenly sky background was a perfect find for pages to honor a church. Choose papers that relate to the location, keeping

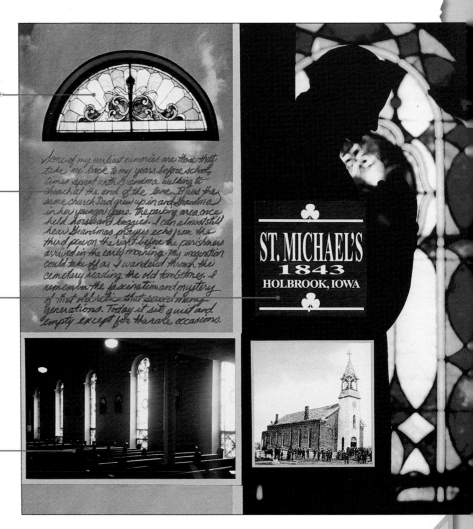

Include photos of architectural details.

Handwrite personal memories.

Use large voids in photos to inset headlines and small important photos.

Photograph artifacts that have special meaning to you.

A visit back to a childhood church inspired these peaceful pages.

in mind that the background paper should enhance, not overpower, the photos.

When photos include a lot of color, mount them on neutral papers before adhering them to the background. The dark area in the large photo on the left-hand page provided a perfect spot for the computer-generated headline. To get this look, print words in white type on a black background so the headline appears to be printed directly on the photo.

Notice that an old black and white photo was placed below the headline for special emphasis. This is centered beneath the headline to maintain an organized layout.

Mount photos on a neutral color of paper to separate them from the background.

Choose a background paper that sets a mood for the pages.

Sand Castles

WHAT YOU'LL NEED
- *Two 12-inch squares of watercolor background paper (Karen Foster)*
- *Crafts knife*
- *Scissors*
- *Ruler*
- *White opaque marker (EK Success)*
- *Seashells*
- *Glue pen; white glitter*
- *Adhesive*
- *Photos*

A glorious day at the beach is pure inspiration for these sun-kissed pages. The watercolor scrapbook paper provides the perfect background for beach photos. These photos show a mix of people, birds, and seashells that tell the story, so little journaling is required. The variety of photos and the distance from which they were taken make this page work beautifully.

The orderly alignment and spacing between the photos keep the layout consistent. The photos at the top center are aligned, while the far left and far right photos are aligned along the bottom.

Use small seashells to add dimension.

Choose a watercolor background paper with smooth warm/cool blended colors to carry out the beach theme.

Use several face sizes to provide interest and variety.

A glorious day at the beach, aqua-blue water, sparkling white sand, and soft warm sunshine inspired these carefree summer pages.

The angled, along-the-edge, and silhouetted photos balance each page. For photos that extend to the edge of the pages, adhere one to the lower edge and one to the upper edge.

To silhouette the bird or seashells, cut very closely around the edge of the object using a crafts knife or small scissors.

The closeup of shells explains the activity in the adjacent picture. For interest, glue real shells in place. When using dimensional objects, such as shells, choose those that lie close to the page.

For the journaling, use a white opaque marking pen to create freestyle curved writing. Retrace the lines with a glue pen and sprinkle with white glitter. Let the glue dry.

Retrace the journaling with a glue pen and sprinkle it with glitter.

Arrange photos with the direction of the faces looking outward or toward the center of the spreads.

Crop some photos as silhouettes.

Las Vegas

WHAT YOU'LL NEED

- *Computer and printer*
- *Colored pencils in yellow, yellow-orange, and orange*
- *Two 12-inch squares of white background paper*
- *12-inch square of map-print paper (Hot Off The Press)*
- *Two 12-inch squares of cloud-patterned vellum paper (Wubie Prints)*
- *12-inch squares of American money printed paper (Wubie Prints)*
- *Press-on gems (Stampa Rosa)*
- *Border line stickers (Mrs. Grossman)*
- *Die-cut Eiffel Tower (Deluxe Cuts)*
- *Vacation mementos, such as show ticket stubs and 3-D glasses*
- *Scissors; adhesive; photos*

Use colored pencils to color in a computer-generated headline.

Overlay map paper with cloud vellum to subtly screen it.

Celebrate friendship and fun with a spread devoted to both. Whether you take a vacation with a friend or enjoy a special outing, capture it in photos to treasure always.

This fun-in-the-sun spread starts with two 12-inch-square pieces of white paper. Because the theme of this vacation is Las Vegas, money paper is a playful choice. Select papers that coordinate with your own travel location.

Cut ½-inch vertical money paper strips and adhere to both pages along the outer edges, allowing a thin strip of white to show along the edge. Next add the map paper, cutting one sheet in half and trimming it, again leaving white showing along the outer

Capture the excitement of a fun, on-the-go vacation with a layout that includes a sunny headline, blue skies, and the hint of a map.

edges. Apply cloud printed vellum over the centers of the page, covering the map areas. Trim as needed.

To cover the edge of the map paper and to create a horizon line, adhere a border line sticker over the vellum.

To create the headline, use a bold outline computer font and print it on white paper. Use colored pencils to color in the letters, using the lightest color on top and graduating to the darkest at the bottom. Carefully trim out the letters along the black lines.

Print out photo captions using the same font as the headline in black. Frame each caption box with a thin black rule, print, and cut out.

Glue the photos, die cuts, mementos, captions, and headline in place. Add gems and silhouetted pieces from the patterned paper.

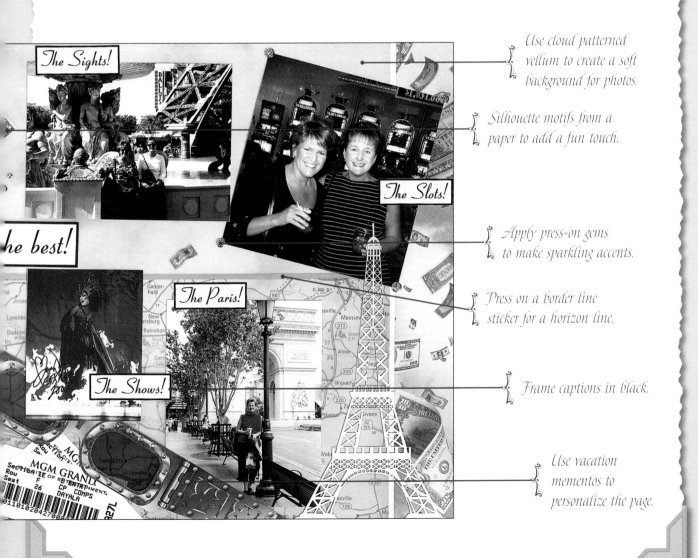

Use cloud patterned vellum to create a soft background for photos.

Silhouette motifs from a paper to add a fun touch.

Apply press-on gems to make sparkling accents.

Press on a border line sticker for a horizon line.

Frame captions in black.

Use vacation mementos to personalize the page.

The Sights!

The Slots!

he best!

The Paris!

The Shows!

The Big Apple

WHAT YOU'LL NEED

- *Tracing paper*
- *Pencil*
- *Scissors*
- *12-inch squares of quadrant papers in yellow and red tones (The Paper Loft)*
- *Green card stock*
- *Gold marking pen (EK Success)*
- *Alphabet stickers*
- *Adhesive*
- *Photos and memorabilia*

The Big Apple is cleverly symbolized with a graphic background element on this travel page. Keep this technique in mind when planning scrapbook pages, using other symbols to subtly state a place, animal, instrument, item, or topic.

To make the apple, enlarge the patterns, *opposite*, 135 percent on a photocopier. Cut out the shapes. Trace around the apple on the red quadrant paper and the leaf on green. Trace around the stem pattern on white paper and color in with a gold marking pen. Cut out the shapes and glue to the background paper, aligning the seams of the two quadrant papers.

Arrange the photos, show stubs, or other memorabilia on the page. Crop the photos and glue them in place. Add sticker lettering and a bolder type for the headline.

Use quadrant papers for a graphic effect.

Mount photos at angles to enliven the arrangement.

Include memorabilia, such as ticket stubs, menus, or maps.

Align the seams of the quadrant papers for an organized appearance.

THE BIG APPLE

New York, New York

Sabbatical

WHAT YOU'LL NEED
- *Two 12-inch squares of blue background paper (Paper Adventures)*
- *Papers for borders and headlines (Karen Foster)*
- *Paper cutter*
- *Crafts knife*
- *Computer and printer*
- *Beige paper for printer*
- *Red marker*
- *Adhesive*
- *Photos*

When putting together an entire album of a subject with several categories, a layout of this nature works well. For these pages, the best photos were chosen from the collection and used as boldly and as large as possible. Titled *Sabbatical,* this brief summation is an enticement to the rest of the album that includes three trips. Each segment is separated by headlines, such as Serengeti and Galapagos.

Notice that the headlines each have a look that fits the region. The main headline, Sabbatical, is set apart in a block of copy created on a computer. The other headlines are cut from paper and applied to the background. If you choose to do this type of

Enlarge candid photos for a dramatic effect.

Balance the overall color in the layout by placing identical colors across the spread.

Inset photos in open spaces of larger photos.

layout, choose ways to distinguish the main headline from the sub headlines.

To make a pattern for each of the headlines, choose bold chunky computer fonts. Print each word in reverse (mirror image or flipped horizontally). Using spray adhesive, adhere the desired colored paper to the back of the printed word. Cut out the letters and adhere to the background paper or on contrasting paper.

Several complementary colors frame these photos. Remember to take your photos to the scrapbook store when choosing paper colors. You may be surprised at the choices you make when you have your photos with you.

These photos range from extreme blue to bright red to dull brown. A wide variety of colors can sometimes cause a page to look off-balance. Notice how the frame colors tie the layout together.

Create a journaling focal point, such as this S, by using an outline computer font with a shadow. Color in the letter with a marking pen.

Turn captions around corners for interest.

Generate headlines on a computer, print backward, adhere to colored paper, and trim out.

SABBATICAL

In 1971, I took sabbatical leave from the University of Missouri to study a tropical grassland system in the Serengeti Plains of Tanzania, East Africa. Among the abundant wildlife were herds of gazelle, wildebeest and zebra, and of course this lion caught closely on camera after a zebra kill. I had the opportunity to climb Mt. Kilimanjaro, a 40 mile walk with 3 huts for overnight stays, the last one being 16,00 feet above sea level.

In the summer of 1974 I enrolled in an extension course which took me to the Galapagos Island to study the flora and fauna. The lack of large predators and humans contributes to the tameness of many animals like this penguin and endemic land iguana. I was easily able to capture this male penguin engaged in courtship display.

In 1978 I spent two months in Europe with Liz and Gary. We visited Stonehenge in England, followed by boat passage across the English Channel, then rail travel to Vienna, Austria, and finished in Czechoslovakia, where I was photographed here on the Polish border resting on a boundary marker.

Norway

WHAT YOU'LL NEED
- 12-inch squares of black card stock
- Mats to coordinate with photos (Die Cuts With A View)
- Paper cutter
- Computer and printer
- Opaque white marking pen (EK Success)
- Adhesive
- Photos

When you have several colorful photos, a black background anchors the images. This Norway vacation spread is a good example of this type of layout.

Because knitted items were some of these vacationers' favorite finds, one of the scarves they purchased during their trip was photocopied and used on the page. The label was included to record the manufacturer. Keep this technique in mind to include stores, places, or other information in your design.

To frame your photos, coordinate mats with photos that go together when placed on the same page or facing pages. Glue the photos to the mats and trim around them if necessary, keeping

Use a computer to make journaling a breeze.

Photograph a favorite purchase for added memories.

Overlooking the tiny town of Myrdal

The colorful houses of Bergen

Looking out the train near Oslo

*Family travels bring back some of life's best memories.
Capture your favorite times together with scrapbook pages
that are reminiscent of the trip.*

frame size widths equal. Computer generate labels and
mount them in the same manner. Tuck the labels under the
framed photos.

To create the headline, use a white opaque marking pen on
bright paper. Here a silhouetted photo adds to the charm of the
headline that is overlapped by paper money.

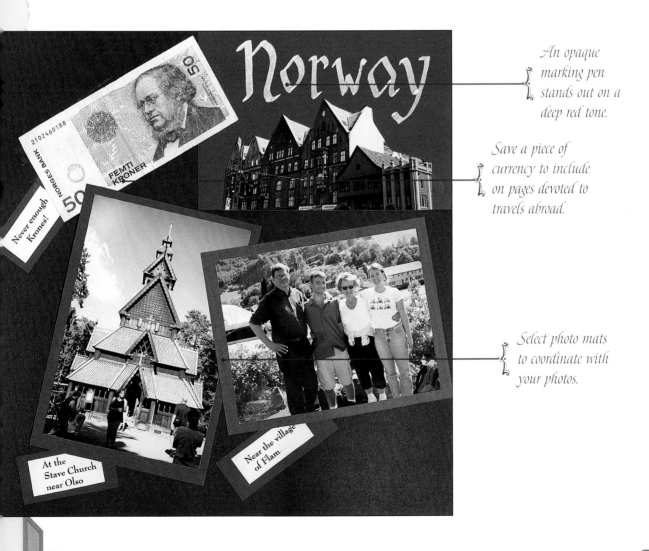

*An opaque
marking pen
stands out on a
deep red tone.*

*Save a piece of
currency to include
on pages devoted to
travels abroad.*

*Select photo mats
to coordinate with
your photos.*

America the Beautiful

This beautiful background of amber waves of grain makes a warm backdrop for these vacation photos that span trips across the United States.

These designer papers are on *pages 175–177*. Photocopy the items at reduced or enlarged sizes to suit your needs. To make the background paper on *page 175* cover a 12-inch-square page, enlarge it 111 percent on a photocopier. The mat bars, star boxes, and journaling box are provided full-size.

The side bars of blue with white stars are mirror images. To achieve this, photocopy one bar from *page 177* at 111 percent, then photocopy a second bar using a mirror or flip setting on the copier.

Overlap photos, being careful to only cover up uninteresting areas.

Use star art for photo corners and as accents.

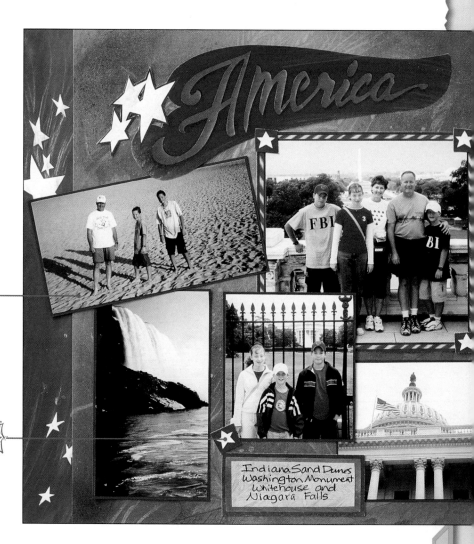

Indiana Sand Dunes
Washington Monument
Whitehouse and
Niagara Falls

*Wherever you travel in the United States, these exclusive papers
will enhance your vacation photos with a display of American pride.*

To make the photo mats, photocopy several striped bars and trim using a crafts knife. Place the strips around the photo, trimming to fit. Glue star squares to cover the corner seams. Use solid papers to mount some of the photos to prevent the layout from becoming too busy.

Cut out the headline, journal box, and additional star squares. Arrange the photos and art elements, overlapping some components and covering open space in photos to add to the interest of the layout. If possible, silhouette a photo image, such as the Statue of Liberty, to overlap the headline.

Add journaling using a marking pen.

CREATE
THESE PAGES
USING OUR
EXCLUSIVE PAPERS
ON PAGES 175
AND 177.

This leaf and grain paper is available on page 175.

Place the headlines at slight angles as though made from a fabric banner.

Make a reversed photocopy of the side banner for a mirror image.

Statue of Liberty
NY City
Alana, Daniel & Aaron
at Accadia Nat. Park

SISTERS

Grandma's Cookies

(my favorites!)

Kitchen Parade

got

I can't believe they're taking photos!

Nice bird!

What is this stuff?!

Who's a turkey?

I AM!

TURKEY?

Stylish

looking back at fond memories

When you acquire vintage family photos, you'll realize that you are holding your family's history in your hands. These precious pictures may tell of your heritage or of fascinating stories of yesteryear. Do these one-of-a-kind photos justice by finding them a place of honor in a scrapbook. This chapter offers wonderful ideas to show off those prized, time-honored photos with papers and scrapbooking treatments that have everlasting appeal.

Richard and Sally

WHAT YOU'LL NEED

- *12-inch squares of patterned background paper*
- *Antique-style decorative-edge scissors*
- *8-inch square and 4-inch round ivory paper doilies*
- *Photocopies of vintage items*
- *Ivory parchment paper*
- *Lace-style border stickers*
- *Disappearing ink pen*
- *Ruler*
- *Black fine-line marking pen*
- *Adhesive; photos*

Whether black-and-white vintage or colorfully contemporary, family portraits deserve a place of honor. These pages focus on the faces of a father and mother and their firstborn son.

The photo crops were determined after the paper doilies were chosen. Look at each doily center to determine how much edge you would like showing. Experiment with a variety of crop sizes on scrap paper before cutting a photograph. If necessary, use a straight pin to remove any cutout areas of the doilies that remain attached. To adhere the doilies to background paper and to prevent damaging the delicate paper, spray each back with a light coat of adhesive.

Make the initial letter larger than the journaling.

Use a ruler and a disappearing ink pen to mark straight rules for journaling.

Crop photos using decorative-edge scissors to fit on a doily. Size by cutting paper scraps to fit the doily.

A lace sticker border softens the hard edge of the parchment paper column.

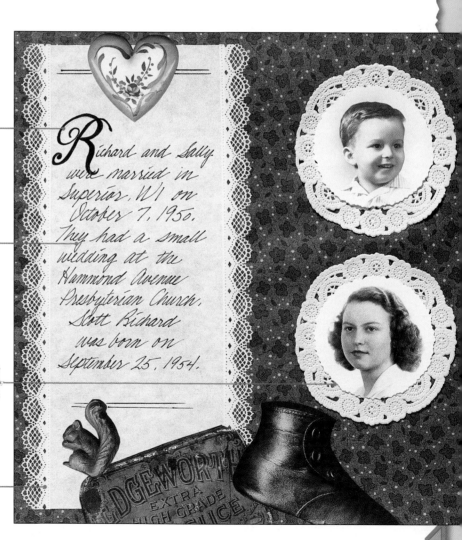

Richard and Sally were married in Superior, WI on October 7, 1950. They had a small wedding at the Hammond Avenue Presbyterian Church. Scott Richard was born on September 25, 1954.

Family portraits bordered in paper lace and photocopied keepsakes are showcased in this endearing display. With plenty of room for journaling, you can include names, dates, or other pertinent information.

To add interest and color to the pages, include photocopies of small family heirlooms, such as this porcelain heart box lid and bronze animals. Silhouette the items to use as embellishments around the photos. These particular metal and glass objects were chosen for their size, shape, and color and arranged in a pleasing manner. Angle the items and adhere some close to the edge of the background paper.

Add a column of journaling to record names and important information, such as birthdates, addresses, favorite memories, or other highlights. Frame the handwriting by drawing rules at the top and bottom with a marking pen.

To cut a small silhouette, move the paper rather than the scissors for a nice clean edge.

Use a pin to remove any cutout areas of the doilies that remain intact.

A fleck of ivory in the background paper coordinates well with the ivory lace accents.

Photocopy metal and glass items to highlight the design.

Grandma's Cookies

WHAT YOU'LL NEED
- 12-inch squares of white background paper
- Vintage kitchen towel
- Five patterned background papers to coordinate with towel (Paper Patch)
- 8½×11-inch piece of white paper
- 8½×11-inch piece of parchment paper
- Wooden fork and spoon (toy size or full-size kitchen utensils)
- White crafting foam
- Recipes on cards
- Silver alphabet stickers
- Scissors; adhesive; photo

This grandma, well-known for her delicious baking, is shown with two favorite cookie recipes. The background that ties the pages together is made from three patterned papers cut into strips and glued horizontally across the pages. A white border frames the pages and acts as a relief from the background patterns.

The vintage paper with the marching characters is actually a kitchen towel that was photocopied in color. The characters on the right-hand page were photocopied using a mirror image setting to allow them to face the characters opposite. These characters were silhouetted and are anchored on a straight baseline.

Place a single photo prominently under the heading.

Choose colorful photo mats that separate the photo from the towel-print background.

Photocopy a vintage kitchen towel to make a unique paper background.

Celebrate the cook in your family and those favorite recipes with a clever page surrounded by motifs from a vintage kitchen towel.

If you don't have a vintage towel on hand, check antiques stores and flea markets for a towel or piece of vintage fabric. Reproductions also are available at discount and fabric stores.

To maintain the patina on the recipe cards, photocopy them in color and trim them to maintain the worn corners.

To create headlines, adhere silver alphabet stickers on white paper trimmed into rectangles. Mount the lettering to one of the patterned papers and trim it ⅛ inch beyond the white. Mount the headline to parchment paper and trim it with decorative-edge scissors.

Cut the portrait into an oval and double mat it. Photocopy a toy wooden spoon and fork. Silhouette the pieces and mount them to strips of foam to make them stand out on the page. If using full-size wooden utensils, reduce the size to fit the page.

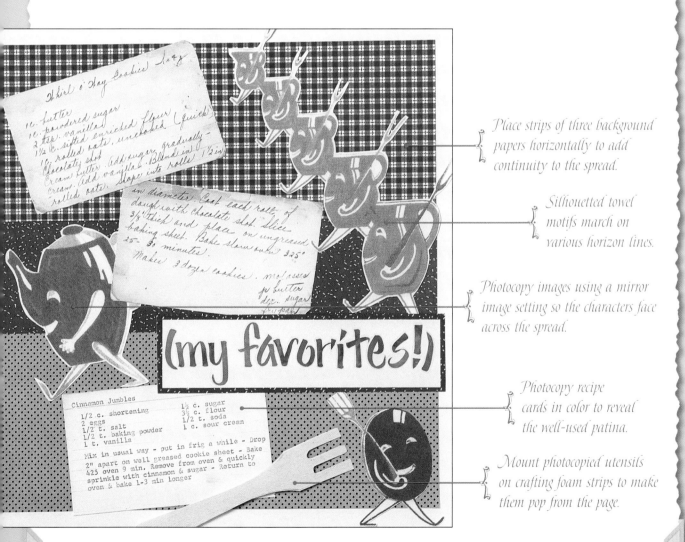

Place strips of three background papers horizontally to add continuity to the spread.

Silhouetted towel motifs march on various horizon lines.

Photocopy images using a mirror image setting so the characters face across the spread.

Photocopy recipe cards in color to reveal the well-used patina.

Mount photocopied utensils on crafting foam strips to make them pop from the page.

Our First Home

WHAT YOU'LL NEED
- *12-inch squares of patterned background paper (Francis Meyer)*
- *Patterned paper for journaling (K & Co.)*
- *Dark green card stock*
- *Fern stamp*
- *Ink pads in two shades of green*
- *Paper cutter*
- *Alphabet stickers (K&Co.)*
- *Key die cuts (Deluxe Cuts)*
- *Adhesive*
- *Photos*

Buying a house and making it a home is indeed a special event. Record the moment, whether it happened many years ago or recently, with meaningful pages for yourself and future generations.

When creating such a spread, it sometimes works best to run the headline across both pages. Alphabet stickers make this process quick and easy.

To balance the pages, place vertical paper bands along the outer edges. Depending on the size and shape of your photos, leave space around each one or overlap some slightly, being cautious of what is covered.

Randomly stamp green card stock with a fern stamp and cut to make photo mats.

Place vertical paper panels on the outer edge of each page to create balance.

Bud and Darlene after a family reunion in 1942.

Bud and Darlene's first home (above) was a one-room country schoolhouse that had been moved to the farm as a dwelling. The war restricted building, so instead of adding on two rooms as planned, only one room and a half basement was added on before Bud and Darlene moved in. The owners put in new windows, doors, and hardwood floors. Neighbor women helped wallpaper and paint. The farm was owned by Equitable of Iowa, as the previous owners had succumbed to the depression on the droughts of the 1930s. They lived here for two years, hauling water from the neighbor's well as theirs was poor. They had no phone or electricity at this home.

Their second rental farm (house shown below) was privately owned, and the house had six rooms. They then lived southeast of Fontanelle for four years before they purchased their current farm in 1948.

*Capture the magic of an ancestor buying a first home with
this charming layout, complete with keys and records of the event.*

The extensive journaling on these pages is divided into blocks to keep the pages organized and easy to read. Handwrite, type, or print the journaling using a vintage-looking font. Leave a border around the copy, trim it, and glue it on each page.

Key and keyhole cutouts work with the house theme. Arrange and glue these elements in place after the photos and journaling papers are arranged. Other elements that may work for this type of theme are mailboxes, house numbers, fences, doorknobs, flowers, and architectural details.

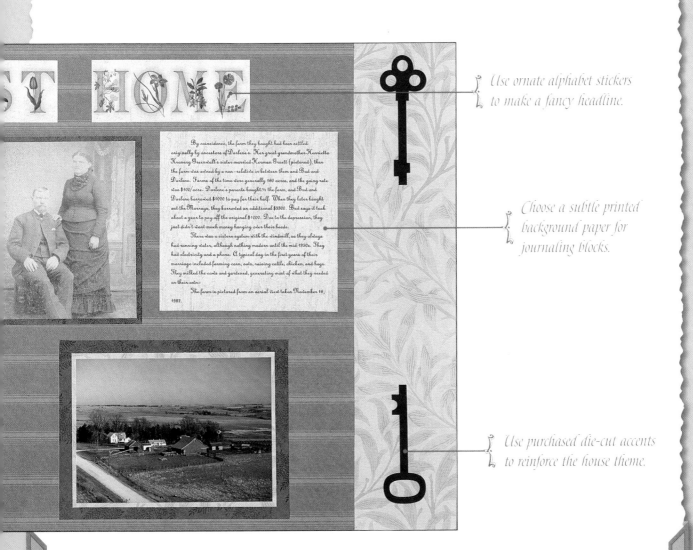

*Use ornate alphabet stickers
to make a fancy headline.*

*Choose a subtle printed
background paper for
journaling blocks.*

*Use purchased die-cut accents
to reinforce the house theme.*

Grandmother

WHAT YOU'LL NEED

- *12-inch square of parchment paper*
- *Rub-on or sticker lettering in large and small sizes*
- *Vanishing ink pen*
- *Buttons*
- *Press-on gems (Stampa Rosa)*
- *Buttons*
- *Thick white crafts glue*
- *Black and white photo in vintage mat*
- *Colored pencils*
- *Hat box, advertising, magazine, store bag, or other item relating to the time period, to be photocopied*
- *Adhesive*
- *Photo*

A formal photo is dressed up even more when softly colored and embellished with gems and fancy buttons. To color a black-and-white photo, use slightly dull-pointed colored pencils. Lightly color in cheeks and lips with a blush color. Add a blue eye shadow color to eyelids. Depending on the photo and the dress, color in details to bring attention to them.

The diagonal band behind this photo is a photocopy of a hat box lid. Achieve a similar look using vintage advertising.

To transfer lettering, draw a guideline using a vanishing ink pen. Use a dull pencil to rub over the letters to transfer them to the paper. Carefully peel off the plastic sheet. To add emphasis to the first letter in the headline, embellish it with press-on gems.

For added sparkle, press on gems and pearls. Glue buttons in place, covering buttonholes with press-on gems.

Apply press-on vintage font lettering for journaling.

Photocopy a vintage hat box or other advertising piece to use as a background banner.

Use press-on gems and pearls to add sparkle to the design.

Sift through a button box for vintage buttons to glue to the photo mat.

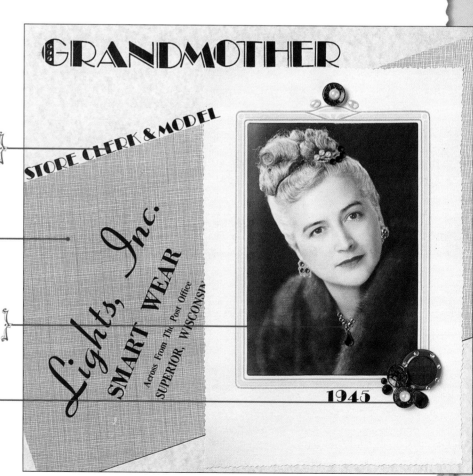

Skating in 1969

WHAT YOU'LL NEED
- 8½×11-inch pieces of black, blue, red, and dotted vellum
- Two 8½×11-inch pieces of white paper
- Computer and printer
- Paper cutter
- Snowflake sequins in red and white
- Clear seed beads
- Beading needle
- White thread
- Adhesive
- Photo

Moms know the trick to wintertime warmth is layering, and this presentation follows the lead. With black paper as a base, white, blue, and red papers are layered over it.

To make the headline and journaling, type them on a computer and print them on vellum. Trim the vellum to fit inside the red background. Cut 1-inch-wide white paper strips and glue on the red, positioning them to highlight the headline and journaling.

Cut a 1¼-inch-wide strip from red paper; glue vertically behind photo. Trim ends to fit within copy. Mount to a white rectangle trimmed slightly larger than photo. Adhere the photo to vellum.

Position the vellum over the paper and tack in place by sewing snowflakes and beads randomly over background. Knot on the back.

Space dots between numbers to make the date the same length as the title.

Adhere red paper vertically to the white mat.

Sew snowflake sequins on paper and hold in place with tiny seed beads.

Overlay dotted vellum for a snowy appearance.

Layer background papers to frame the page.

Print the headline and journaling on the vellum overlay.

SKATING
1 • 9 • 6 • 9

Sue getting ready to head to the Red Barn Ice Rink for some figure skating!

Honorable Duty

WHAT YOU'LL NEED
- *Tracing paper*
- *Pencil*
- *Scissors*
- *12-inch square of parchment paper*
- *12-inch squares of red and blue textured-looking papers (Two Busy Moms)*
- *8½×11-inch pieces of vellum*
- *Computer and printer*
- *Star paper punch*
- *⅛-inch-wide double-stick tape*
- *Round black shank buttons with star inserts (Le Bouton)*
- *Thick white crafts glue*
- *Wire cutters; vintage-style decorative-edge scissors*
- *Photocopies of war-related items, such as letters, medals, papers, books, diaries, etcetera*
- *Adhesive; photos*

A waving flag in the background sets the stage for pages devoted to military service. To re-create the look, enlarge the patterns, *opposite*, at 670 percent. Cut out the pieces and trace onto red and blue papers. Cut out the blue corner and red stripes. Using the pattern as a guide, glue the pieces on parchment.

To make the bold headline, choose a bold font with serifs. Type the word DUTY in all capitals to the right of the page, approximately 1¾ inches high. Center the word HONORABLE above DUTY in smaller type, sizing to fit the length of the word. Print the headline on vellum. Trim smaller than the background so that the flag borders the vellum. Use a star-shape paper punch to

Use star buttons for a hint of patriotism.

Punch stars between the letters for detail.

Choose a bold computer type and print on vellum to allow the flag motif to show through.

A subtle flag waves in the background of these scrapbook pages that honor a family members' service in the military.

punch a row of five stars between the letters of DUTY, plus one at the beginning and one at the end of the word. Adhere the vellum to the background using double-stick tape along the edges.

Remove the button shanks using wire cutters. Glue the star shapes into place. Glue the buttons to the left of the lettering.

Trim the photos with decorative-edge scissors. Trim all other pieces with straight scissors. Glue the items in place, allowing important dates, words, and insignias to remain visible.

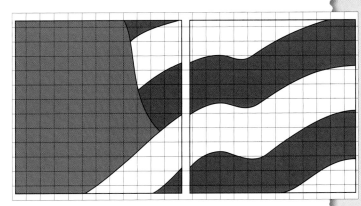

FLAG PATTERN   1 SQUARE = 1 INCH

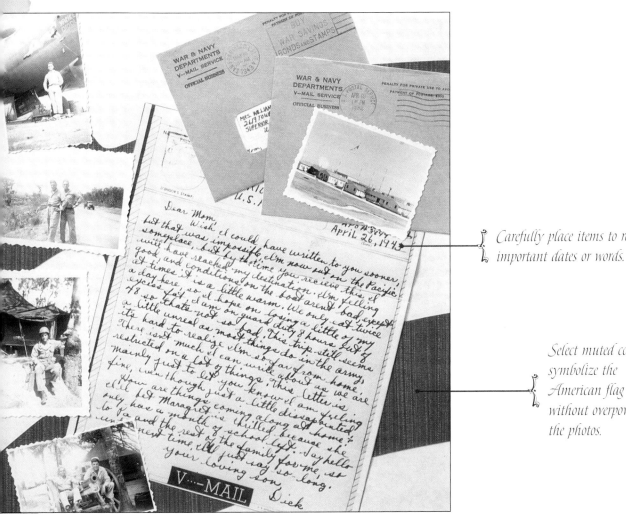

Carefully place items to reveal important dates or words.

Select muted colors to symbolize the American flag without overpowering the photos.

Brothers

WHAT YOU'LL NEED

- 12-inch squares of burgundy paper (Colorbök)
- Red polka-dot paper (Colorbök)
- Red striped paper (Colorbök)
- Tan linen paper (K & Co.)
- Sheer ribbon
- Paper tags (Paper Reflections)
- Chalk
- Rub-on ivy, morning glory, and hummingbird motifs (Scrapbook Borders)
- Paper cutter
- Computer and printer
- Adhesive; photos

A single headline, flanked by sprigs of ivy, tells the story of these siblings. These examples include a symmetrical page on the left and an asymmetrical page on the right.

Create layered photo mats using a combination of striped and polka-dot papers. Crop the photos and glue them to the striped paper. Trim and mount them on polka-dot paper. Trim again.

Add the ivy, hummingbird, and morning glory designs, overlaying ivy along the edge of a mat or headline.

Chalk the edges of the tags, embellish, and tie a sheer ribbon through each of the tags.

Print the headline in dark green to coordinate with the ivy.

Cut 12-inch-square paper to 8½×11 inches to fit through a printer.

Turn striped paper vertically and horizontally for interesting photo mats.

Use rub-on motifs as decorative elements on each page.

Sisters

WHAT YOU'LL NEED

- 12-inch square of patterned plum background paper (Making Memories)
- 12-inch square of lavender velvet embossed paper (K & Co.)
- 8½×11-inch green, plum, and lavender floral paper (Déjá Views)
- 8½×11-inch lavender and metallic gold print paper
- Periwinkle floral stickers (Stickopotomus)
- Plum precut mat (Making Memories)
- 1-inch-wide sheer green ribbon
- Scissors
- Paper cutter
- Decorative-edge scissors
- Alphabet stickers (Provo Craft)
- Adhesive
- Photo

Luscious colors and dainty details frame this black-and-white photo of happy-go-lucky sisters. This page involves a few trims and a little bit of layering.

Mark a 10¾-inch square on the back of the velvet paper and cut out using decorative-edge scissors. Adhere to the center of the background paper. Tape the photo behind the precut mat. Mount to the lavender and gold paper. Trim ¼ inch beyond the edge of the mat. Mount this paper on the green patterned paper and trim ½ inch beyond the edge. Adhere this layer 1 inch from the top of the velvet paper.

Press lettering on the lavender paper and mount it on metallic-gold and lavender paper. Trim to the width of larger mat. Trim the top and bottom. Add floral stickers and a ribbon bow.

Use sheer ribbon so it will lie flat when the scrapbook is closed.

Use die-cut stickers to add lovely floral accents.

Make framing a breeze with a purchased mat.

Use adhesive stickers to make a simple headline.

Use decorative-edge scissors for a vintage look.

John & Dorothy

WHAT YOU'LL NEED

• *Papers or photocopied papers from page 179*
• *Cream and ochre-color papers*
• *Computer scanner and printer or photocopier*
• *Paper cutter*
• *Crafts knife*
• *Scissors*
• *Straightedge*
• *Adhesive; photo*

Easily create a page similar to this with your own special photo and floral art from *page 179*. Solid tan and ochre-color papers were used in combination with the art provided.

Cut the cream-color paper approximately ¼ inch smaller than the ochre background. Center and glue it in place.

To create the photo mat, trim the paper mat from *page 179* and adhere it to a piece of ochre-color paper. Trim the ochre paper to create a narrow outline of color on the outside and in the opening. Place the mat over the photo and glue in place with the journal box. Copy two sets of the photo corners, one at 100 percent and one at 50 percent. Cut out the corners and finial; glue them in place. Also on *page 179*, you'll find art for additional photo corners and finials.

CREATE THIS PAGE USING OUR EXCLUSIVE MAT AND FLORAL ART ON PAGE 179.

Choose solid colors to coordinate with your photo.

Affix the trimmed floral frame over the solid color, then trim edges with crafts knife and straightedge.

Use colored marker to coordinate with the artwork.

Choose from three sets of floral art on page 179.

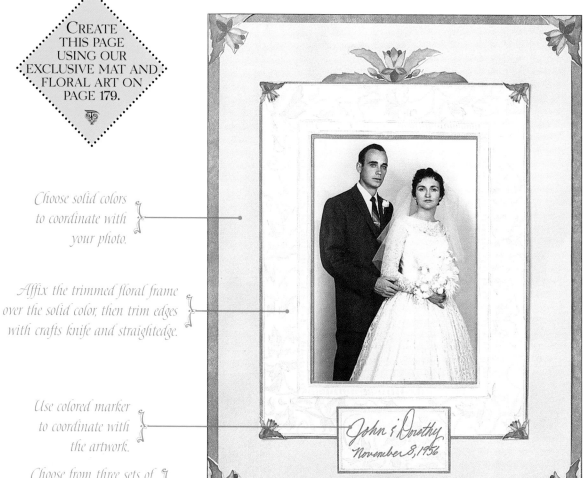

John & Dorothy
November 8, 1956

The Little Flower

WHAT YOU'LL NEED

- 12-inch square of background card stock
- 12-inch square of vellum
- Embossed paper with frames (Francis Meyer)
- Computer, printer, and colored paper
- White opaque marking pen
- Crafts knife
- Adhesive
- Photos

This special memory and an unfamiliar story was documented for this Grandmother's descendants. Photos were few and the one shown here is special. If you have stories in your family and few photos, stretch your imagination to portray something relevant and emphasize the special photo that you have.

This story is about a grandmother and a yellow rosebush that played an important part in her early married years. The rosebush still exists, so some photos were taken in order to complete the story and the page. The beautiful background photo was enlarged on a photocopier. To soften a photo like this, apply a sheet of vellum over it. To create a gentle headline, use an opaque marking pen to write the words.

Use adhesive between photo and vellum only where it will be covered by the narrow mat.

Write the title using an opaque marking pen.

Frame the story using solid papers.

Cut a romantic oval mat to flatter a vintage photo.

Enlarge and print background photo as large as possible.

Emphasize a small closeup photo by placing it prominently and flowing the type beside it.

the Little Flower

In 1930, Grandma Emma Kucera was a Christian mother who prayed faithfully expecting answers. The yellow rose was symbolic of Saint Theresa, also called "The Little Flower", who was symbolic of answered prayer. Grandma and Grandpa had a difficult time searching for a home for their new family during these depression years. They came upon a farm with glorious abundant flowers and among them were the yellow roses. She knew this was an answer to her prayers. It became their home, as well as home to her descendents to this day. The yellow rose still grows there as well as the homes of her children and grandchildren around the country.

Grandpa and His Music

WHAT YOU'LL NEED

- 8½×11-inch piece of neutral music-note paper
- 12-inch square of vintage-looking neutral background paper (The Family Archives)
- Music-staff charms; pliers
- Black photo corners; glue stick
- Large black music-staff die cut (Deluxe Cuts); toothpick
- Medium-tip metallic gold marking pen
- Gold press-on lettering
- Fine-tip black marking pen
- Clear adhesive for metal
- Adhesive; photo

Three stories are told by this rare photograph: a grandpa's love for music, his love for his dog, and his dog's love for music. Even though the photo is not of high quality, it is a cherished keepsake to include.

This music-related theme is carried through by papers, charms, and a paper cutout. Trim the papers to the desired sizes and adhere them to the background.

To remove the rings at the top of the charms, carefully bend back and forth using a needlenose pliers. Glue in place using a small amount of clear adhesive applied with a toothpick.

Press down the headline lettering. To draw the border, hold a ruler in place and draw lightly with a black marking pen ¼ inch from the edges, allowing the marking pen to miss areas for a worn appearance. Repeat with a rule of gold pen ⅛ inch from the edges.

Draw rules to guide handwriting.

Glue metal charms to the page to add sparkle and dimension.

Draw a light rule around the page for a vintage look.

Use a die cut to reinforce the theme of the page.

Got Turkey?

WHAT YOU'LL NEED

- 2 coordinating 8½×11-inch pieces of reversible paper (Westrim Crafts)
- 8½×11-inch piece of white paper
- Scissors
- Crafts knife
- Self-adhesive brown paper leaf shapes (Canson)
- Orange-brown colored pencil
- Blank photo caption stickers
- Fine-line black permanent marking pen
- Metallic gold alphabet stickers
- Adhesive: photos

When sifting through photos, we often find ourselves saying, "Why in the world did I take THAT?" Don't toss out those images too quickly; they may be perfect for a scrapbook page. These old photos are great examples.

These photos are perfect for photo captions. To avoid errors, write the words on the sticker before placing it.

Coordinating reversible papers (olive-green tones were a natural choice here) work great for making photo windows. Cut out a mat leaving a corner intact, and glue back the flap. Use white for the borders to keep the elements from blending in with the background.

Paper leaves carry out the autumn theme on this page, but you could choose any die-cut shape to reinforce a theme.

Use photo caption stickers to add a lighthearted touch.

Cut windows in reversible paper for interest.

Clip corner of the photo diagonally.

Accent photos and headline with a white border.

Highlight the leaves with strokes of colored pencil.

Make the lettering pop by adding a marking pen shadow under and to the right of each letter.

Liljander

WHAT YOU'LL NEED
- *Tracing paper; pencil*
- *Crafts knife*
- *Straightedge*
- *Transfer paper*
- *Tape*
- *Two 12-inch squares of white card stock*
- *11½-inch squares of light blue textured papers (Sweetwater)*
- *8½×11-inch piece of brown patterned paper (Sweetwater)*
- *12-inch squares of three or more green patterned papers (Paper Patch)*
- *Paper cutter*
- *Computer and printer*
- *Photocopies of items*
- *Black fine-line marking pen*
- *Adhesive*
- *Photos*

With a family name boldly stated in a headline and a tree shape on the opposite page, there's no doubt that this is an honored selection from a family tree.

To make the tree, enlarge the patterns, *page 100*, at 200 percent on a photocopier. Cut out the large shape. Draw around the shape in the center of blue paper. Carefully cut out the tree shape using a crafts knife and a straightedge.

Using transfer paper, transfer the cutout patterns to the center of white paper. Cut out the windows using a crafts knife.

Cut green paper slightly larger than the window shapes and tape them in place on the back. After two of the patterns are

Use a computer to generate a pattern for the headline.

Use paper scraps to make photo corners.

Crop, layer, and glue to make quick photo mats.

Elmer Gust Liljander

Born—June 22, 1902
Married—December 12, 1925
to Lilah May Elsmore
born September 25, 1901
Children—Sally Marie Liljander
born December 1, 1928

Lilah May

Elmer Gust

Record your family tree with photos, lifetime highlights, and photocopies of important personal items.

symmetrically positioned, place a third green paper behind the cutouts to fill in the remaining areas. Tape brown paper for the tree trunk on the back of the white cutout. Tape the cutout tree under the blue cutout piece. Glue these layers on white paper.

To create a family name headline, print out the name. Transfer the letters to white paper and cut out using a crafts knife. Tape brown paper beneath the cutout letters. Glue to the page. Cut triangles from green papers for corners.

Crop photos as desired. Glue each photo to a background paper. Trim just beyond the photo. Add more mats if desired.

Type and print journaling in the same font as the headline.

Mount on a single paper in the same manner as used on the photo mats.

Photocopy and crop items in silhouette style. Glue components in place, and add handwritten journaling in black marking pen.

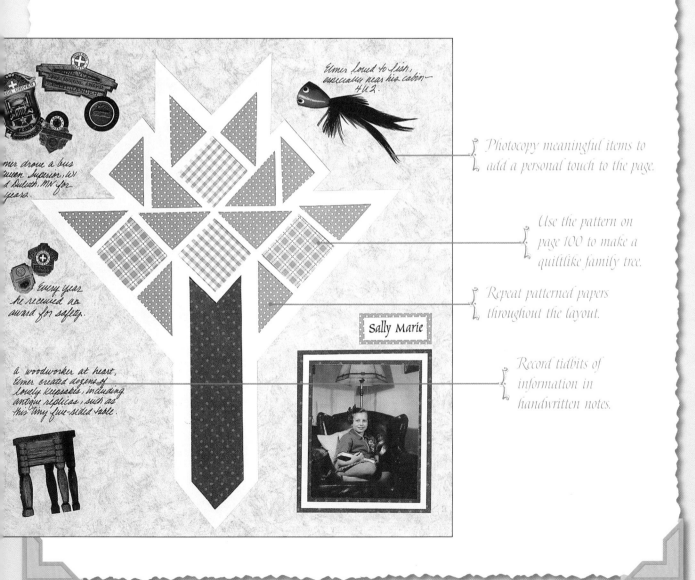

Elmer loved to fish, especially near his cabin— 4U2.

mer drove a bus tween Superior, WI d Duluth, MN for years.

Every year he received an award for safety.

a woodworker at heart, Elmer created dozens of lovely keepsakes, including antique replicas, such as this tiny five-sided table.

Sally Marie

Photocopy meaningful items to add a personal touch to the page.

Use the pattern on page 100 to make a quiltlike family tree.

Repeat patterned papers throughout the layout.

Record tidbits of information in handwritten notes.

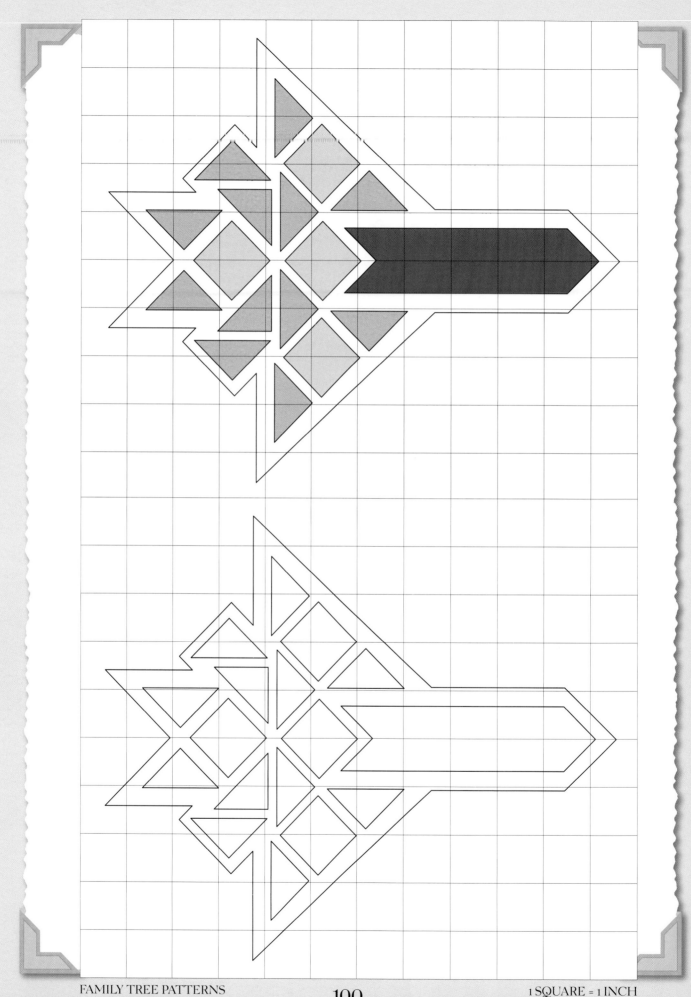

Kids of the '60s

WHAT YOU'LL NEED

- *Camera*
- *Cherished items, such as a storybook, old watch, harmonica, jump rope, airplane, slingshot, paddleball, jacks, billfold, dolls, or other toys*
- *Photocopier or computer, scanner, and printer*
- *Patterned paper for title*
- *Black-and-white photos*
- *Brown background paper*
- *White paper*
- *Gray translucent paper*
- *Decorative-edge scissors*
- *Black marking pen*
- *Adhesive; photos*

Gather your childhood photos, toys, books, greeting cards, or other items related to an era. Combine them to make these fun memory pages.

To create the background papers, arrange favorite items from childhood in a rectangular area, placing the most important items around the edges because photos will cover most of the center area.

Photograph your items laying flat. To make the final paper appear screened back so that it doesn't appear overly colorful and overpowering, do a creative enlargement either on your computer or on a photocopier. If you have a computer available, you may be able to scan and lighten the image. Or use a photocopier and light control to alter the colors.

Trim the photos, mount them on white paper, and trim the border paper with decorative scissors to resemble photos printed from the '60s. To create a shadow effect, cut gray translucent paper with the same scissors.

Choose an appropriate paper to print a computer-generated title.

Arrange items and photograph them for a one-of-a-kind background.

Cut shadows from gray translucent papers.

Handwrite journaling with a black marking pen.

Use decorative scissors to trim white squares.

Dad's Stamps

WHAT YOU'LL NEED

- 12-inch squares of solid background paper
- 12-inch square of postage stamp paper (Anna Griffin)
- 12-inch square of vellum
- Photocopy of stamp book cover
- Line border stickers (Mrs. Grossman's)
- Colored paper scraps
- Postage stamp-related cutouts (Fresh Cuts)
- Decorative-edge scissors with a postage stamp edge pattern
- Eyelets in desired colors and shapes, eyelet tool, paper punch
- Leather lacing in desired colors
- Vellum envelope
- Nonvaluable postage stamps
- Black marking pen
- Adhesive; photos

Whether it's postage stamps, handmade pottery, or vintage cars, many of us love collecting something. These scrapbook pages incorporate a photo of the man who obtained the stamps, a photograph of his children admiring his work, bits of the collection itself, and theme-related papers and art.

Because postage stamps are so colorful, the photographs here are used in black and white to stand out from the intricate artwork of the stamps. This neutral tone balances the pages. Silhouetting the man on the right-hand page gives the photo importance and ties him to the headline, "Dad's Stamps."

Apply adhesive strategically so the top cutouts cover the marks.

Use vintage-looking cutouts to add interesting shapes and postmarks.

Apply line stickers in colors that coordinate with the stamp paper to define and secure the vellum edge.

A labor of love is captured on these nostalgic pages.
Real stamps are mixed with purchased paper accents for scrapbook
pages that capture bits of history and a passion for collecting.

To tone down the postage stamp paper used to enhance the page, a square of vellum covers the center portion, allowing the border to remain bright and in focus. This same technique is used on the right-hand page as stamps peek from a vellum envelope. Some of the paper cutouts are backed with solid paper so they stand out among the collection of stamps.

Tags cut from paper scraps help group a sampling of stamps, and a larger tag is used as a background for the headline. The tags and one of the photo mats were trimmed using decorative-edge scissors that resembles the perforation of a postage stamp. Little details like this make a page outstanding.

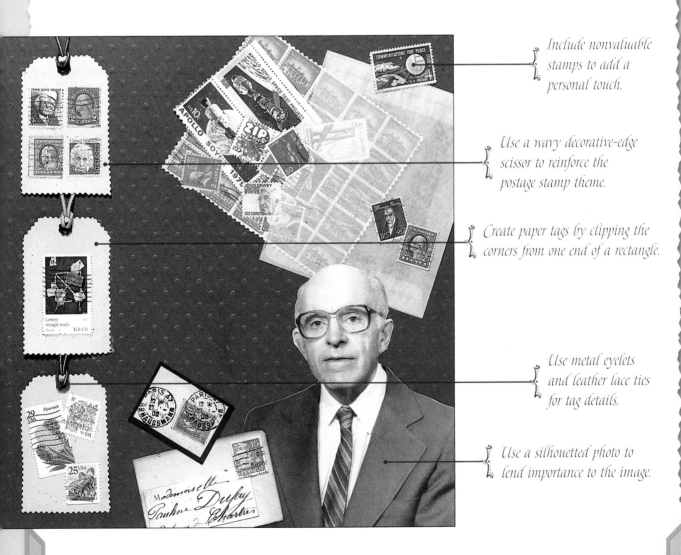

Include nonvaluable stamps to add a personal touch.

Use a wavy decorative-edge scissor to reinforce the postage stamp theme.

Create paper tags by clipping the corners from one end of a rectangle.

Use metal eyelets and leather lace ties for tag details.

Use a silhouetted photo to lend importance to the image.

Growing Up

WHAT YOU'LL NEED

- Two 12-inch squares of neutral card stock for background
- Embossed wallpaper border
- Brown shoe polish (liquid or paste)
- Clean rag
- Black paper
- Alphabet stickers in black and gold
- Brown textured paper
- Black fine-line marking pen
- Crocheted lace
- Buttons
- Wire cutters
- Pearls
- Thick white crafts glue
- Adhesive: photos

S epia tones, black, and white reflect the vintage appeal of these five photos. To add the embellishments, you need not look any farther than a button box.

To make the leather-looking vertical bands, cut two 12-inch-long strips of embossed wallpaper border. Use brown shoe polish on a rag to color the strips; let them dry. Glue the strips aligned with the outer edges on the background papers.

To mount the photos, trim them to size and mount them on black paper. Trim the paper slightly beyond the edge of each photo. The arrangement balances well here, placing a large photo on the left page and four small photos on the right. If your photos are

Layer gold lettering over black to create an instant shadow.

Apply shoe polish to a wallpaper border to create a rich texture.

Rich leatherlike banners and delicate lace, buttons, and pearls add dimensional beauty to these candid black and white photographs.

irregular sizes, arrange them until the two pages seem to balance. Glue the photos in place.

The journaling pieces are created by tearing a square and a rectangle from brown textured paper. Write the photo captions on the paper pieces using black marking pen. Add black around the torn edges, allowing it to bleed slightly. Glue in place.

Use black alphabet stickers for the title on the left-hand paper, tipping the letters to the left and right. Position the gold letters on the black and slightly lower and to the right.

Glue the lace, buttons, and pearls in place using crafts glue.

Use snippets of lace, buttons, and pearls for vintage charm.

Tear textured paper and ink the edge for old-looking paper pieces.

William and Meta

WHAT YOU'LL NEED

- 12-inch squares of background paper
- Patterned paper (Hot Off the Press)
- Colored card stock
- Flower and fern punches (Plaid Enterprises, EK Success, and Martha by Mail)
- Glue dots: tweezers
- Scissors: silk flowers
- Moiré fabric
- Dark green suede paper
- Fiber (On the Surface)
- Bow template (Deja Views)
- Chalk (Craf-T)
- Photo corners (Stickopotomus)
- Adhesive: photo

Flowers are a perfect fit for any wedding photo, antique or new. This wonderful vintage photo is right at home surrounded by paper and silk bouquets.

To make the flowers in the lower right-hand corner, punch out various size flowers from card stock. Immerse the punched pieces in water for a few seconds and then crumple the pieces into small balls. Partially uncrumple the balls and let them dry. Arrange the handmade flowers on fern designs and glue in place. For dimension, use glue dots to adhere the flowers in place.

For the upper left-hand bouquet, use a small bundle of silk flowers, found in the wedding section of a crafts store. Create a paper bow using a template. Chalk the edges to create a shadow. Glue the pieces in place, including a fiber behind the journal box.

Use a template to create a bow for the bouquet.

Make a mini bouquet using tiny silk flowers.

Use moiré fabric as an appropriate wedding accent.

Make tiny paper blooms to add to the vintage theme.

William Meyer and Meta Ihnen
February 4, 1914

Stylish

WHAT YOU'LL NEED
- Two 12-inch squares background paper
- Red suede paper
- Chalk (Craf-T)
- Pop dots
- Gel pen (Pentel)
- Circle punch (EK Success)
- Colored paper
- Adhesive
- Photo

This clever apparel presentation dresses up any ordinary scrapbook page, especially one that includes a vintage portrait. You can re-create the look here or study your photo and adapt the design to mimic the look of the photo.

To create the collar, cut a line 5 inches down the center of one paper square. Fold back the inside corners as a collar and hold in place using adhesive dots. Add shadowing to lapels using chalk.

To make the buttons, punch circles in red suede paper. Chalk the edges and add white gel pen highlights. Glue in place. Cut and add suede details as desired.

Mount photos and journaling on suede paper. Chalk the edges of the journaling paper. Position the pieces on the jacket like pockets. Mount the jacket on background paper.

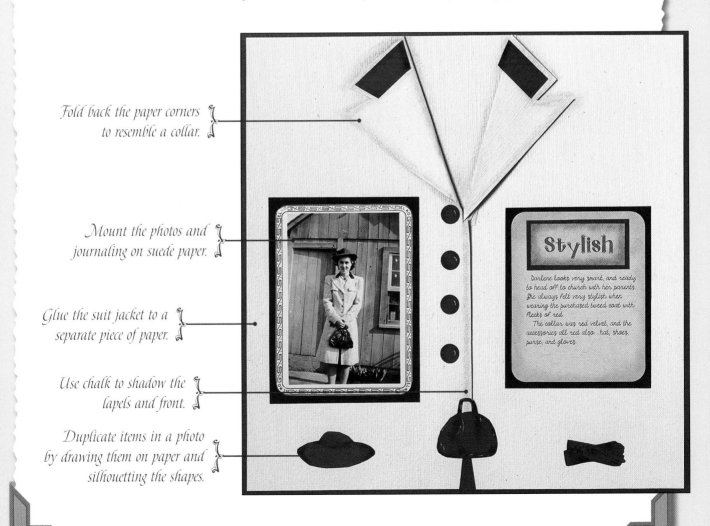

Fold back the paper corners to resemble a collar.

Mount the photos and journaling on suede paper.

Glue the suit jacket to a separate piece of paper.

Use chalk to shadow the lapels and front.

Duplicate items in a photo by drawing them on paper and silhouetting the shapes.

Stylish

Darlene looks very smart, and ready to head off to church with her parents. She always felt very stylish when wearing the purchased tweed coat with flecks of red.

The collar was red velvet, and the accessories all red also: hat, shoes, purse, and gloves.

celebrating holidays and special occasions

Gathering together in celebration, no matter what the occasion, is always guaranteed to bring smiles. This fun chapter travels the seasons to bring you delightful ideas to transform your photos into keepsake pages. Whether you have photos that capture little ones searching for Easter eggs or Christmas photos that beg to be placed on festive scrapbook pages, now's the time to make the most of your photos that mean so very much.

Four Little Pumpkins

WHAT YOU'LL NEED
- *12-inch squares of card stock in black, green, and yellow*
- *Orange paper with black dots (Paper Patch)*
- *Pumpkin cutouts (Stamping Station)*
- *Black paper fence*
- *Alphabet punches (EK Success)*
- *Chalk (Craf-T)*
- *Foam Squares (Therm-O-Web)*
- *Adhesive*
- *Photo*

With black and orange as the primary colors on this page, you know Halloween fun is in store. This fence idea works perfectly for photos taken at a pumpkin patch or during jack-o'-lantern carving.

For the background, trim the orange dot paper to reveal a black border. Add a crescent moon, pumpkin cutouts, the fence, and spiky green paper grass. To make the fence appear old, brush it with lines of chalk.

Silhouette a photo and mount it on black paper. To make it pop from the page, back it with foam squares. Adhere the photo at the top of the fence.

To make the headline, use alphabet punches. Glue in place in three wavy lines over the paper moon.

Cut a paper moon to shine beneath the lettering.

Use alphabet punches to make a headline quick and easy.

Choose a background paper with a small pattern to add texture without distracting from the photo.

To create dimension, mount a photo on card stock and foam squares.

Rub the fence with chalk to give it an aged appearance.

Bobbing For Apples

WHAT YOU'LL NEED

- *12-inch square of orange scrapbook paper*
- *Apple*
- *Knife*
- *Acrylic paints in red and green*
- *Disposable plastic plate*
- *Lime green paper*
- *Letter stamping set; ink pad*
- *Patterned paper*
- *Decorative-edge scissors*
- *Adhesive; photos*

Apple prints make an ideal background for any autumn occasion. To make a print, cut an apple in half. Put red paint on the plate. Referring to the photos, *right*, dip the apple in paint and stamp it on the background paper. Let dry. For leaves, cut a leaf shape from the other half of the apple. Dip the shape in green paint and stamp at each apple top. Let dry.

Glue photos on papers; trim; adhere to background. Stamp headline on paper. Trim headline and black strip with decorative-edge scissors.

Cut the headline and black paper strip using decorative-edge scissors.

Use stamps to make a bold headline.

Use patterned papers to add interest to the edges of the photos.

To avoid high contrast, use orange paper for the background.

Stamp the apple prints randomly on the background paper.

Boo!

WHAT YOU'LL NEED
- Polka-dot paper or photocopy of paper on page 181
- Solid papers in black, lime green, and yellow
- 12-inch square of lavender background paper
- Tracing paper
- Pencil
- Crafts knife
- White colored pencil
- Permanent black marking pen
- Scissors
- Dimensional spider, web, and pumpkin stickers (EK Success)
- Stitched appliqué letters to spell "BOO!"
(available in the notion section of fabric and discount stores)
- Thick white crafts glue
- Adhesive; photos

It's fun to record Halloween costumes worn through the years. The design on this page enables you to include the dress-up choices for one year or several.

The page is created from the papers on *pages 181 and 183*. The house provides window and door openings that are just the right size to silhouette trick-or-treaters. To make the house, photocopy it from *page 183* and cut it out using a crafts knife. Cut the door opening along the dotted line and fold the door open. Highlight the house with a white colored pencil. Cut lime green paper to fit behind the house.

Choose the moon cutout of your choice from *page 181*. The ground paper and mini cutouts also are on that page. (Photocopy them so you can use them over and over!)

The photos on this page are relatively the same scale; you can reduce or enlarge them to get the same effect. Use small scissors to crop the silhouettes.

Use Halloween stickers and stitched appliqué letters to add the eerie finishing touches to this hauntingly happy scrapbook page. If using spider stickers with strings, tack down the string with a dot of crafts glue.

Tack strings in place using a dot of thick white crafts glue.

Trim the web to fit in the corner of the page and use the discarded pieces to trim the windows.

Use white colored pencil to create highlights on the left and underside of house features.

Fold open the door to create another photo placement area.

Use stitched appliqués found in the notion section of fabric stores to make lettering easy.

CREATE THIS PAGE USING OUR EXCLUSIVE PAPERS ON PAGES 181 AND 183.

Capture the spirit of Halloween with a bright and playful haunted house design. This vibrant page combines ready-made papers with quick-design stickers to concoct wonderfully "terror-ific" detail.

Christmas Past

WHAT YOU'LL NEED

- *12-inch squares of Christmas paper (K & Co.)*
- *Christmas stickers (K & Co.)*
- *Colored card stock (DMD)*
- *Tree die cut (All My Memories)*
- *Assorted fibers (Cut It Up)*
- *Star brads (Magic Scraps)*
- *Double-stick tape (Art Accents)*
- *Glitter accents (Art Accents)*
- *Crafting wire*
- *Eyelet tool; paper punch*
- *Gold heart eyelet (Persnippity)*
- *Stocking die cut (Creating Keepsakes)*
- *Alphabet punches (EK Success)*
- *Adhesive; photos*

These Christmas pictures captured not only ear-to-ear smiles but also the styles of the time. To make a holiday layout, choose a festive yet subtle holiday paper for the background.

Crop all of the photos into squares and use multiple mats for framing. Use holiday stickers to dress up the photo mats in a hurry.

Wrap the die cut tree with a fiber garland. Attach a star brad to the top of the tree.

To make the headline, punch it from card stock using alphabet punches and place it to span both pages. To balance the right page,

Attach a wire hanger to the corner of a paper die cut to make it into an ornament.

Wrap a die cut tree with decorative fiber and place a star brad at the top.

Holiday photos from the early '70s rekindle the joy that only Christmas brings. Surround the snapshots with festive motifs to add to the fun of those Santa Claus days.

place three star brads after the word "past." For sparkle, apply double-stick tape across the top of the words and add glitter. Punch the numbers for the year and place them vertically on the lower half of the left page between the photo and the tree.

Create journaling to fit in a stocking-shape die cut. To make it appear as an ornament, punch a hole in the corner and attach a heart eyelet in the hole. Bend a wire hanger and secure it through the heart eyelet. Loop the wire around the "A" in Christmas.

Create the Christmas packages using scraps of paper tied with fiber bows. Glue small packages beneath the tree and two large packages on the right-hand page.

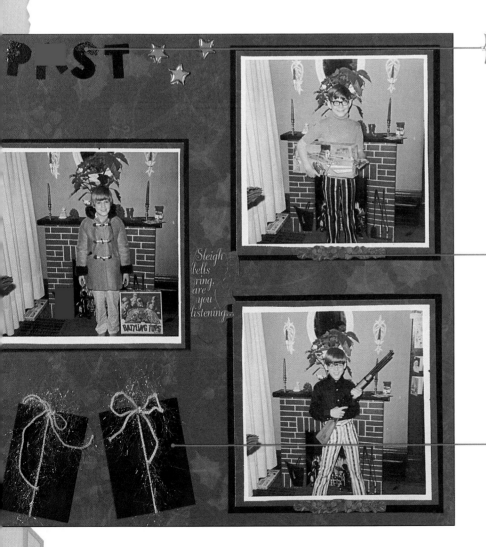

Hold glitter accents in place with double-stick tape.

Use stickers to make decorative corner accents and mat details.

Tie fiber bows around paper packages to create dimension.

Naughty or Nice

WHAT YOU'LL NEED
- 12-inch square of dark green paper
- Paper cutter
- Papers in red and gold
- Holly rubber stamp
- Embossing ink pad or slow-drying green or clear pigment ink pad
- Embossing powder in green or clear; embossing heat tool
- Gold marking pen
- Green gel pen
- Adhesive
- Photos

Adapt this layout to any grouping of photos you have of the same subject with different expressions. To keep this page from becoming monotonous, the photo sizes are varied intentionally, placing three small ones trailing down to the last large one for impact. To frame the photos, mount them on red paper, then on gold paper.

To emboss the background, stamp your image using an embossing ink pad or a slow-drying green or clear pigment ink pad. Sprinkle the stamped image with green or clear embossing powder. Shake off the excess powder. Heat the images with an embossing heat tool to melt the powder onto the background paper. Draw the headline using a gold marking pen and embossing gel.

Use a gold marking pen and embossing gel for a quick headline.

Vary photo sizes, angles, and expressions to keep the page interesting.

Use a gel pen for subtle color.

Layer mats in holiday colors to add pizzazz to the page.

Use a rubber stamp and embossing gloss gel to create a textured background.

Christmas Recipe

WHAT YOU'LL NEED
- *Background paper*
- *Mat papers*
- *Scissors*
- *Holiday stickers*
  (me and my BIG ideas)
- *Recipes*
- *Fine-line marking pen*
  (EK Success)
- *Adhesive; photos*

Gather a batch of yummy holiday recipes, blend with a handful of favorite photographs, add a pinch of green and red, and include some traditional holiday motifs for a holiday booklet recipe you can complete in an evening.

This fun combination of ingredients makes it easy to fill the pages, especially when the pages are small. With a white background, the photos, mats, and stickers are all that's needed to make each page interesting. Simply arrange and adhere the components for each page in the most pleasing manner.

Photocopy recipes, reduced if necessary, to fit a small page format.

Include personal memories about the photos and recipes.

Make your pages any size desired.

Holiday stickers add an instant merry touch.

Use mats in Christmas colors to add to the holiday theme.

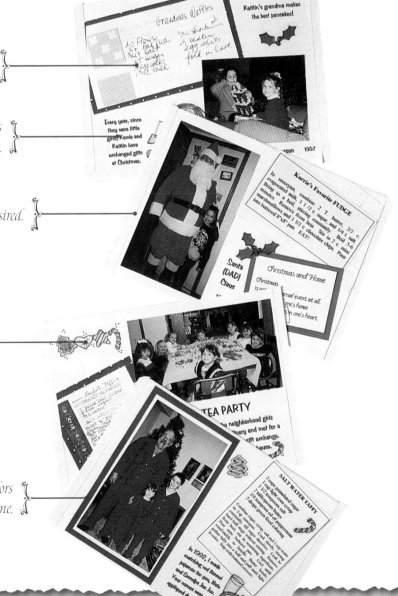

Season's Greetings

WHAT YOU'LL NEED

- *12-inch squares of background paper*
- *12-inch square of dark red paper*
- *Silver patterned paper (Paper Adventures)*
- *Bonbon-size foil baking cups in red, pink, silver, and turquoise (Wilton)*
- *Silver Season's Greeting die cut (Griff's Shortcuts)*
- *Clear beaded trim (Hirschberg Schutz & Co., Inc.)*
- *⅛-inch-wide double-stick tape (Suze Weinberg's Wonder Tape)*
- *Metallic silver snowflake stickers*
- *Turquoise paper*
- *Silver alphabet stickers (Provo Craft)*
- *Vintage Christmas note cards (available in antiques stores or use reproductions)*
- *Vellum*
- *Paper cutter*
- *Adhesive; photos*

New or old, holiday photos capture happy times of the season. Combine your holiday photos with vintage note cards, foil, and bead trims for a spectacular presentation.

To create a page spread with this vintage appeal, start with the top banner. Cut red strips about 3¼ inches wide and glue ⅛ inch from the top edge of each page. To add the foil accents, first flatten out baking cups with your fingers. To scallop the border, cut pieces from the foil circles. Glue pink scallops across the top and red scallops across the bottom of the red paper strip. Glue silver foil scallops across the bottom of the page.

To add the beaded band, adhere a strip of double-stick tape just below the red paper. Stick the ribbon portion of the trim to the

Use a silver die cut headline for a sparkling start.

Enlarge a photo Christmas card for big impact.

Use numeral stickers to identify the year of a snapshot.

Make your holiday memories sparkle by surrounding cherished photos with beaded icicles, metallic snowflakes, vintage greeting cards, and foil circles reminiscent of antique Christmas tree trims.

tape, keeping it straight. To reduce the bulk when placing the trim under note cards or photos, cut the beaded trim to barely go behind the item.

Enlarge a photo or photo greeting card to fill the space on the left page. Mount it on turquoise paper and trim ⅛ inch beyond the photo. Tuck a red foil circle under the lower right corner and glue it on a larger rectangle cut from patterned silver paper. Glue in place.

Add vintage note cards or Christmas cards under and alongside the photos. If you have a holiday letter available, photocopy it on vellum and attach over an opened note card using snowflake stickers. Date the photos using sticker numerals. Place the date

below the large photo and place the dates in a blank spot on the remaining photos.

Glue all the pieces in place and apply snowflake stickers to add sparkle.

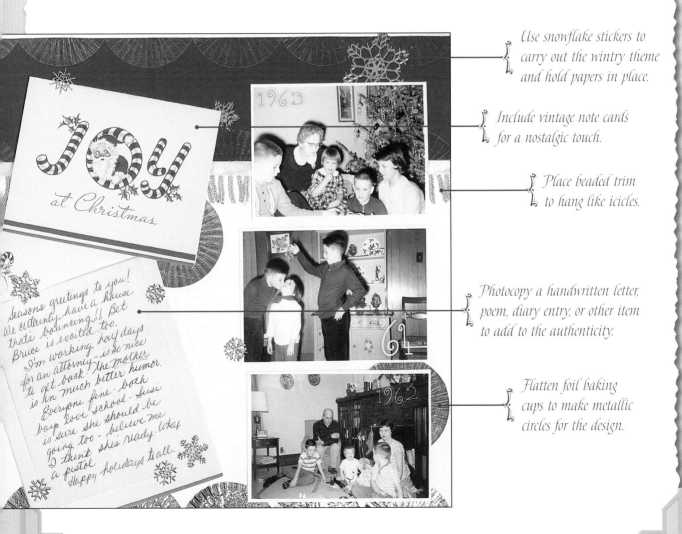

Use snowflake stickers to carry out the wintry theme and hold papers in place.

Include vintage note cards for a nostalgic touch.

Place beaded trim to hang like icicles.

Photocopy a handwritten letter, poem, diary entry, or other item to add to the authenticity.

Flatten foil baking cups to make metallic circles for the design.

Merry Christmas Abby

WHAT YOU'LL NEED
- 12-inch fold-out scrapbook pages (available at scrapbooking stores)
- 12-inch square of ornament-printed paper (Sonburn)
- Red paper (Paper Adventures Paper al fresco)
- Chalk (Craf-T)
- Foam squares (Therm-O-Web)
- Scissors and/or crafts knife
- Ruler
- Paper scrap, tag clip art, or purchased gift tag
- Paper raffia (Paper Adventures)
- Adhesive
- Photos

One glance at this pair of scrapbook pages and you'll know holiday fun is close at hand. These giftwrapped pages fold back to reveal a host of Christmas photos four pages wide.

Once a festive background paper is selected, choose a paper that will stand out to make a giftwrap bow. To make the bow, trace the full-size patterns, *page 122*, onto tracing paper. Cut out each pattern and trace around it on the back side of the bow paper. Carefully cut out the bow using scissors or a crafts knife. The straight ribbon portions can be cut using a paper cutter or a ruler and crafts knife.

To make the gift tag, use one you create or use a purchased tag. When printing a tag on a computer printer, decide on the size and

Cut ribbon from paper strips to make the pages appear wrapped.

Shade the edges of a gift tag with chalk.

Whether you want to add divider pages to separate your scrapbook themes or create a wondrous top sheet to fold back and reveal a special collection of photos, this merry package idea is perfect for the holidays.

type in the lettering. Cut out the tag. To soften the look of the tag, apply chalk around the edge.

To adhere the bow and ribbon in place, mount on foam squares to add dimension. Use raffia to tie the tag onto the bow. Glue the tag in place.

{RIGHT} *The two pages open up to reveal four pages of photos inside.*

} *Mount the bow with foam squares for dimension.*

} *Choose an ornament-laden paper that resembles holiday giftwrap.*

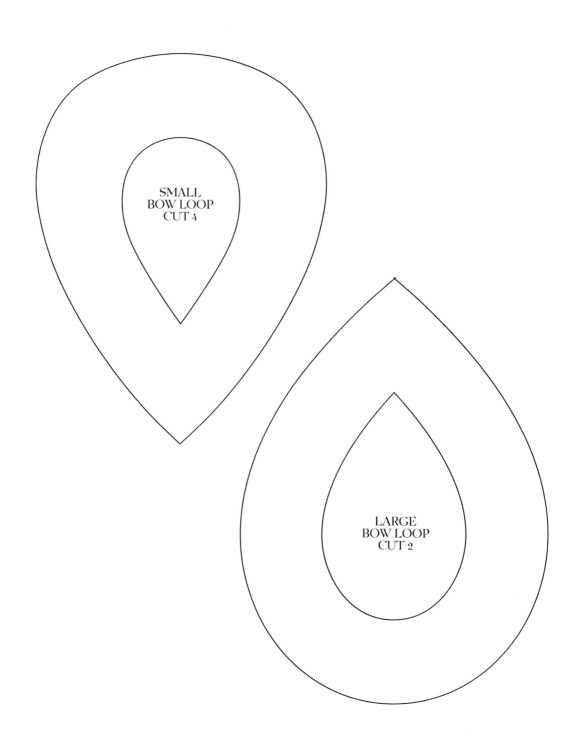

SMALL
BOW LOOP
CUT 4

LARGE
BOW LOOP
CUT 2

Graduation Day

WHAT YOU'LL NEED
- *Photocopy of paper on page 185*
- *12-inch square of background paper*
- *Colored marking pens*
- *Crafts knife; paper cutter*
- *Adhesive; photos*

CREATE THIS PAGE USING OUR EXCLUSIVE PAPERS ON PAGE 185.

Honor a graduate with a page like this, customizing the background with class colors and unique journaling. The mats and headlines found here are provided in black and white on *page 185*. Scan or photocopy these art pieces and color them in with marking pens. You can reduce or enlarge these art elements to create your page.

A pastel paper worked well with this graduate's strong yellow and red school colors. Before choosing background paper, you may wish to color in the designs and mount your photos. Bring those elements with you to select paper.

To lay out a page like this, keep it clean and balanced to recognize such an important event.

Create your own year with the numbers from page 185.

Use school colors to personalize the black-and-white mat design.

Enlarge the best photo to draw the most attention.

Personalize a mini diploma to capture the importance of the day.

Happily Ever After

WHAT YOU'LL NEED
- Two 12-inch squares of patterned coordinating papers (Anna Griffin)
- Vellum
- Paper cutter or crafts knife and ruler
- Ivory lace adhesive border (Mrs. Grossman's Paper Co.)
- Embossed ivory paper (Anna Griffin)
- Solid papers in burgundy and ivory
- Decorative corner paper punch
- Alphabet stickers
- Adhesive
- Photos

The nature of these wedding photos called for a formal approach on this spread. For the elegant background, two coordinating papers were chosen. The common deep red hue creates compatibility between the pages.

The busier floral pattern is used for a single photo with a wide mat. The monotone background works best for the four smaller photos.

The photo on the left gets special attention being the single focus on the page. The mat is created with an ivory embossed paper placed over a slightly larger burgundy mat. For added elegance, translucent paper was cut into a square and placed on

Use translucent paper, lace, and embossed ivory paper to make beautiful wedding pages.

Choose papers similar to the decor of the wedding to complement the photos.

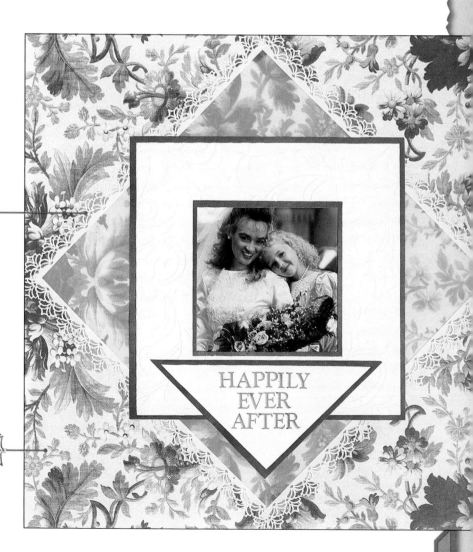

HAPPILY
EVER
AFTER

Relive the joy of a blissful "I do" day with scrapbook pages
that are as elegant as a bride's wedding gown.

point on the page beneath the photo mat. Bordered with adhesive ivory lace, the diamond softens the patterned paper around the photo, making it stand out on the page. A triangle was created in the same manner as the photo mat and a simple uppercase sticker headline was applied.

For the right-hand page, four photo mats were cut from ivory paper. The corners are given a lacy look with a decorative corner punch. The newlyweds' names are center stage in a second diamond shape, using upper- and lowercase alphabet stickers.

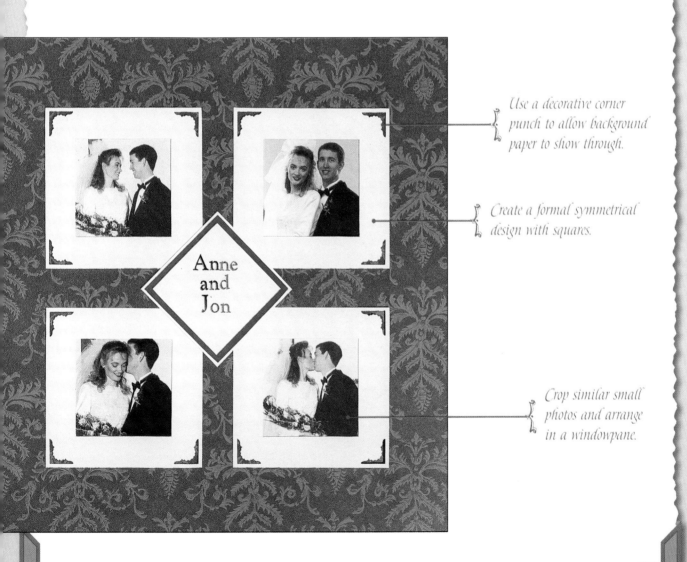

Use a decorative corner punch to allow background paper to show through.

Create a formal symmetrical design with squares.

Crop similar small photos and arrange in a windowpane.

Holy Matrimony

WHAT YOU'LL NEED
- *12-inch squares of parchment paper*
- *Papers in black and rust*
- *Reduced photocopy of vintage marriage certificate on page 187*
- *Enlarged photocopies of marriage certificate for borders and photo mat*
- *Photocopy of black polka-dot papers, felt photo mat, and headline on page 189*
- *Black fine-line and wide permanent marking pens*
- *Scissors*
- *Adhesive*
- *Photo*

With lovely artwork from an 1800s wedding certificate, you can re-create this vintage-looking spread.

To make the pages, you will need three photocopies of the certificate on *page 187*; one reduced at 67 percent, one enlarged at 140 percent, and one enlarged at 220 percent. On the reduced photocopy, trim the certificate and personalize the blanks using a marking pen. On the 140-percent enlargement, trim it as shown on the right-hand page to use as a mat beneath the felt photo mat. The remaining enlargement will be used for the vertical floral strips, headline, and cutout flowers. To create these, outline the desired areas with a wide black marking pen and crop leaving black borders.

Tip a black rectangular paper to create a shadow.

Fill in the certificate on page 187 with family wedding information.

Outline the pieces in black to create a guide and shadow.

Mark and Esther were Susan's great-great grandparents. Mark was related to President Cleveland.

A beautiful marriage certificate from the 1800s provides intricate floral artwork that embellishes these wedding pages.

The felt photo mat, polka-dot strips, and outer triangles can be cut from the full-size elements on *page 189.*

Adhere the polka-dot triangles in the outer corners. Cut ¼-inch-wide strips from polka-dot paper bands. Adhere the strips 1 inch from the bottom of the pages and extending from the centers.

Glue the vertical floral bands on the outer sides of each page. Cut out the headline, mount on black paper, and trim.

Mount the certificate on rust paper and trim. Cut a piece of black paper this size. Glue it at an angle behind the certificate.

Cut out the center of the photocopied mat. Tape a photo behind the mat. Adhere the mat to the certificate on the right-hand page.

Write journaling next to the personalized certificate. Draw a rule above it. Adhere the floral die cuts where desired.

CREATE THESE PAGES USING OUR EXCLUSIVE PAPERS ON PAGES 187 AND 189.

Cut out sections of the enlarged copy of the certificate for floral accents.

Cut out this ready-made mat to frame a special wedding photo with vintage style.

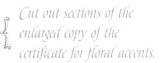

Cut strips of paper to make striking accents.

Family Reunions

WHAT YOU'LL NEED

- 12-inch squares of background paper
- Vellum
- Watercolor pencils (Staedtler)
- Blender pen (Marvy)
- Eyelets (The Stamp Doctor)
- Eyelet tool; paper punch
- Ivy cutouts (Wallies, McCalls)
- Rose stencil (Plaid)
- Scissors
- Photo album pages in desired sizes
- Sewing machine and thread
- Adhesive
- Photos

When you have lots of pictures to include but don't want to devote several pages in your scrapbook, here's a creative way to accomplish the task.

To make each mini flip book, remove pages from a photo album. Stack several sheets and sew them onto card stock using a sewing machine.

Create a computer-generated headline and color it in using watercolor pencils that coordinate with your photos and page theme. Use a blender pen to blend the pencil colors.

For interesting details, add eyelets, ivy cutouts, and a rose stencil. Color in the stencil design with watercolor pencils to tie the color to the headline.

Use eyelets as decorative accents on journaling boxes.

Layer 3-ring binder pages to create mini flip books.

Use watercolor pencils to color in headlines and stencils.

Easter Eggs

WHAT YOU'LL NEED

- 12-inch square of yellow polka-dot paper (Making Memories)
- 12-inch square of green patterned paper (Stamping Station)
- Sticker letters (PrintWorks)
- White card stock
- Oval cutter
- Colored pencils in pink, yellow, and green
- Photocopier or scanner and printer
- Scissors; adhesive; photos

This fun page can be made from different poses you may have of your little ones. You can use one child or many. A number of poses can work with this layout, especially if the subjects appear to interact with each other.

For the ground, cut a wavy strip from green paper and adhere it to the bottom of the yellow background.

Enlarge the photos to the desired sizes and trim around the children. Use an oval cutter to cut shapes from white paper. Zigzag-cut the ovals in two, to appear as a cracked egg.

Decorate the eggs with simple floral motifs drawn with colored pencils inspired by the stickers. Write names on the bottom portion of the eggs using colored pencil. Add the headline, allowing it to slightly overlap an eggshell.

Choose papers to coordinate with the die cut letters.

Position photos to interact with each other to create personality.

Choose a subtle design background paper.

Draw simple designs on eggshells that are inspired by the headline.

Cut a strip of green for the ground to anchor the photos.

Tea for Two Hundred

WHAT YOU'LL NEED

- *Two 12-inch squares of neutral patterned papers*
- *Two 8½×11-inch pieces of red-and-gold formal papers*
- *Papers in navy blue, white, metallic gold, and red*
- *Rubber stamps in teapot, teacup, and spoon designs (Art Impressions)*
- *Metallic gold ink pad*
- *Metallic gold marking pen*
- *Emblem stickers*
- *Paper cutter or crafts knife and ruler*
- *Scissors*
- *Blue fine-line marking pen*
- *Party invitation*
- *Adhesive*
- *Photos*

Looking back at parties will surely bring back happy memories of the day. This yearly tea, brimming with laughter, good food, and great friends, is a grand occasion to capture in scrapbook pages.

Whether you host a tea for two (or 200), a wedding shower, or a holiday party, be sure to share those good times by placing them on scrapbook pages such as this.

To reproduce this formal look, choose your papers carefully. The colors and patterns set the tone for a formal page. Because this is a British tea, red and blue are predominant colors. The red-and-gold center papers appear as one piece when placed next to each other,

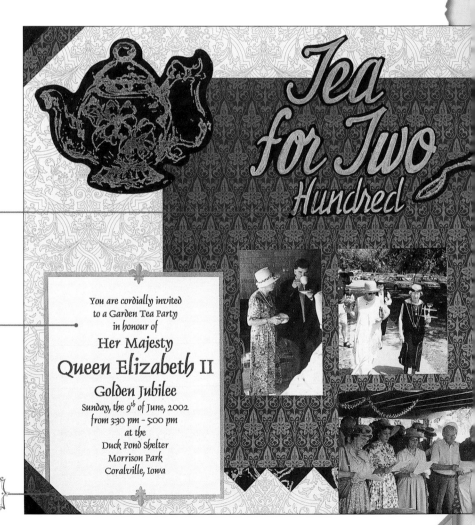

Handwrite the headline in gold ink on blue paper and trim close to the lettering.

Photocopy parts of an invitation to set the stage for the theme.

Choose paper accents to reinforce the colors at the party.

You are cordially invited
to a Garden Tea Party
in honour of
Her Majesty
Queen Elizabeth II
Golden Jubilee
Sunday, the 9th of June, 2002
from 3:30 pm – 5:00 pm
at the
Duck Pond Shelter
Morrison Park
Coralville, Iowa

*A labor of love is captured on these nostalgic pages.
Stamps intermix with purchased paper accents for scrapbook pages
that capture bits of history and a passion for collecting.*

anchoring the many photos on this spread. To carry out the gold color, gold solid paper frames some of the elements, gold ink is used for stamping and writing, and gold stickers are used to help hold the invitation clippings in place.

To create the tea motifs, use rubber stamps and stamp gold ink on blue paper. Trim the pieces just beyond the stamped area. For details, randomly stamp blue paper scraps and cut out to make a lower border and a journal mat.

When arranging your photos, consider whether some should extend off the top, bottom, or sides. On the left-hand page one photo extends off the bottom, while the opposite happens on the

right-hand page. This, along with careful placement of remaining photos, cutouts, and the headline, balances the pages.

Dress comfortably
but appropriately
Ladies: Hats requested
Special Entertainment
beginning at 3:30 pm
R. S. V. P.
Hosted by: Rusty Banker

Incorporate tiny art elements to transform plain boxes into stylish ones.

Stamp navy paper with gold ink to create a formal look.

Russ a self-taught caterer, hosted his first party in 1990. Now hundreds attend the tea.

Stamp extra paper to add decorative details.

4th of July

WHAT YOU'LL NEED

- 12-inch square of white card stock
- Primary-colors card stock mats (Die Cuts with a View Mat Stack)
- Star patterned papers (Die Cuts With A View)
- Computer and printer
- Chalk (Craf-T)
- Star punch (Marvy)
- Adhesive
- Photos

Whether it's watching a parade, honoring the flag, or waving a sparkler in the air—everyone loves the 4th! This page helps you record favorite patriotic moments.

With a white background paper, the primary colors seem to dance on the page. Generate the headline on a computer and cut it out using large zigzag cuts. To add a colorful background, glue red, yellow, and blue squares to the background in a horizontal bar. Center the headline over the squares.

Ready-made mats make framing a cinch. Notice one photo is cropped horizontally and one vertically. These are balanced by the boat silhouette in the lower right-hand corner.

Use colorful stars to act as confetti on the page. Punch them from the same papers used behind the headline.

Print the headline on a computer and trim using random zigzag cuts.

Angle 2-inch paper squares to frame the headline.

Use precut mats to make photo mounting easy.

Silhouette photos to add dramatic interest.

Punch stars from paper scraps for accents.

Celebration

WHAT YOU'LL NEED
- Tracing paper
- Pencil
- White transfer paper
- 12-inch square of black paper
- White dressmaker's pencil
- Cardboard key-ring tag with wire removed
  (available at office supply stores)
- Round template
- Alphabet stickers
- Balloon stickers
- Scissors
- Adhesive: photos

For a whimsical approach to displaying party photos, place photos of your guests' heads on drawn stick figures. To make this fun background, enlarge the pattern, *below left*, 445 percent on a photocopier. (You will have to enlarge it again and again. Ask someone at the photocopy store to assist you.) Trace the design on tracing paper. Place transfer paper between the pattern and black paper; retrace. Draw over lines with a dressmaker's pencil.

The photos on this page are each framed with a purchased key-ring tag. Remove the wire rings. Using a round template slightly smaller than the tag, draw circles around the faces and cut them out. Glue a face in the center of each tag. Glue tags on drawing.

To add the headline, apply stickers in a wavy line, angling to make the lettering lively. Apply balloon stickers and draw strings.

Place alphabet stickers in a wavy line to enliven headline.

Use cardboard key rings to make ready-made frames for head shots.

Draw lines for balloon strings.

Use a dressmaker's pencil on black paper.

PEOPLE PATTERN   1 SQUARE = 1 INCH

mom
the artist

at the table

THE
BUTTERFLY GARDEN

We found the most
beautiful garden
on the Saylorville
bike trail. The
kids were
fascinated seeing
hundreds of
colorful butterflies.

OUR NEW HARLEY

Me and Dad

Summer 2001

Tink
July 1, 2002

enjoying beloved hobbies and pets

We love them, spend time with them, and can even be consumed by them. Yes, hobbies and pets play an important role in our happiness! Now you can devote some extraordinary scrapbook pages to your favorite animals and pastimes. We'll show you more than a dozen approaches to organizing your photos into something terrific. So no matter if you ride a horse or a Harley, love to draw or are drawn to flowers, this page-packed chapter will have you running for your scissors and glue!

Me & My Horses

WHAT YOU'LL NEED

- *12-inch squares of wheat background paper (Wubie Prints)*
- *Paper cutter*
- *Papers in green, gold, and brown*
- *Decorative-edge scissors*
- *Green sticker lettering*
- *Green opaque marking pen*
- *Adhesive*
- *Photos*

Beautiful horses and happy childhood memories make this a memorable layout. Whether your little one has horses or kitties, be sure to take plenty of photos to recall those happy times together.

The wheat background chosen here adds a richness of color without overpowering the photos. The dominant colors in the photos are brown and green, therefore shades of both work well for accent colors. Deep green frames the photos; use a brighter green for lettering and rich brown and ochre for journaling blocks. You may wish to select other colors to coordinate with your photos.

Apply stickers side by side and overlapping for interest.

Use a photo, such as this horse's head, that leads into the layout.

With a love for horses, this little guy is right at home in the saddle. Beautiful photos combined with just the right papers make this a keepsake spread.

This layout packs as many photos as possible into the space. To achieve this look, align the margins neatly along the top, bottom, and sides with narrow spaces between photos. To unify photos, such as the three on the right, mount them on one dark green panel of paper. Notice how the large horizontal photo below it lines up on the sides. The large bold vertical photo on the left is deliberately placed. The direction of the horse's head leads into the rest of the layout and directly into the child's photo.

To create interesting labels, use decorative-edge scissors to cut the paper pieces and mount them on gold paper panels.

Group photos on one panel for extra-quick matting.

Use decorative scissors to create interesting shapes for journal boxes.

Line up edges neatly for an organized appearance.

LUCKY, HERBIE BUCK & GUS

Best Friend

WHAT YOU'LL NEED

- Two 11×8½-inch pieces of green background paper
- Photocopies of paper on page 191
- Scissors; crafts knife
- Metal ruler
- Black fine-line marking pen
- Adhesive; photos

Just the right photo mats, journal boxes, and headlines will help your pet photos shine. The art provided on *page 191* will help you create your own pet page.

Photocopy the desired art elements full size, or reduce or enlarge them to fit your photographs. The inside of the doghouse can be trimmed away and used as a photo mat. To trim straight edges, use a crafts knife and a straightedge, such as a metal ruler.

To add the personalized doghouse sign, trim it from the center of the doghouse art and glue it at an angle for journaling.

Print the name of your dog or dogs to personalize the doghouse.

Use the doghouse art as a photo mat.

Silhouette a single puppy in proportion to the size of the doghouse.

Use a ruler and crafts knife to cut straight edges.

Use a black marking pen to create striking journaling against the watercolor label.

CREATE THESE PAGES USING OUR EXCLUSIVE PAPERS ON PAGE 191.

Tink – July 1, 2002

WHAT YOU'LL NEED
- Four varying shades of green paper (Colorbök, Karen Foster)
- Ivory textured paper
- Paper cutter
- Oval template
- Swivel blade
- Ruler
- Computer and printer
- Paper floral photo corners and die cuts (Stickopotomus)
- Adhesive
- Photo

Carefully choosing just the right colors and papers can give you an elegant look without spending a lot of time.

Before cutting photo mats, layer the papers at the edges and place them over one edge of the photo. Rearrange the papers until you are pleased with the way they enhance the photo.

Create the smallest, oval photo mat using an oval template and swivel blade, leaving at least 1 inch of mat around the photo. Measure and cut the next mat. Allow a border of the first mat to show around the edge. Continue cutting mats to fit under the previous mat. Shift the mats up to allow for journaling. Adhere photo corners. Type the journaling on a computer, adding an oval border. Print it and trim around the oval. Adhere floral trims.

Choose subtle accent papers that do not overpower the photo.

Repeat the oval shape for the journal box below.

Use floral paper embellishments for easy elegance.

Add decorative photo corners as finishing touches.

Tink
July 1, 2002

139

Our New Harley

WHAT YOU'LL NEED

- 12-inch squares of background paper in coordinating colors
- Bike tire
- Black stamp pad
- Orange acrylic paint and paintbrush
- Black paper
- Crafts knife or scissors
- Paper cutter
- Computer and printer
- White or colored paper
- Permanent marking pens
- Adhesive; photos

These fun black-and-white photos create a simple bold spread just by their own nature. To get this look, mount photos on black paper and trim. Create contrast using different colors of paper for the left and right pages. Using black-and-white photos will tie the pages together.

To make the tire tracks, roll a clean and dry tire across an ink pad or paint and then roll across the paper.

Print the main headline in white on a black background. Print the subheads in black on white. Color in the white areas using yellow and orange marking pens.

Use a bold, colorful headline to draw your attention and lead into the main photo.

Use a computer to generate easy-to-read journaling.

Line up the top of headline with top of photo for an orderly appearance.

Trim photos the same size, keeping unity in an asymmetrical layout.

Stamp tire treads on background to create interest and carry out the theme.

Mom the Artist

WHAT YOU'LL NEED

- Variety of colored papers
- Special appropriate paper for border (Provo Craft)
- Watercolor paper
- Crafts knife
- Scissors
- Paper cutter
- Alphabet template: pencil
- Fine-point markers
- Colored pencils
- Adhesive: photos

This artistic page uses colorful elements but is tied together with good design rules. While this page is about a person and her artwork, the design could be adapted for any hobby. You can use this same concept to create a page with a name, title, and pictures of relevant items. Use a variety of sizes and silhouetted shapes to keep it interesting. Choose one particular item to focus on, as was done with the man in the moon. Include one or two rectangular shapes so the design is not overly busy. These, along with the checkered border, help maintain order.

Use different colored marking pens to add journaling, following the silhouetted items. For the title, trace letters using a template and cut them out. Layer the letters over papers of various colors, cut irregular shapes using decorative scissors.

Use an appropriate border paper that relates to the theme.

Layer letters on random colorful paper shapes for a dramatic headline.

Mount a rectangular photo on an irregular mat.

Lightly color in some of open space with colored pencil.

Break into the border with silhouetted photos.

Bath Time Blues

WHAT YOU'LL NEED

- *12-inch squares of patterned paper (Making Memories)*
- *Flannel paper (Paper Adventures)*
- *Lettering template (Provo Craft)*
- *Waterdrop stickers*
- *Oval template*
- *Punches (EK Success)*
- *Fiber (On the Surface)*
- *Vellum (Bazzill)*
- *Adhesive; photos*

When Fido gets his next bath, record it for all to enjoy— even if he doesn't! A catchy headline, cut using a lettering template, sets the tone for this pet page.

Using blue for the background, glue a fiber across the top and bottom. Glue it in a wavy pattern to resemble water.

To separate the photos from the background, mount them on coordinating papers and trim close to the photo edge. Note how these photos are cropped, overlayed, and intermixed with journaling. The journaling, printed on vellum, softens the base paper pattern and makes for easy reading.

To make the headline, cut out the letters and apply them to the top and bottom of the scrapbook page over the wavy fiber pieces.

Separate the words of the headline to frame the top and bottom of the page.

Choose a patterned paper for a bathing theme.

Apply waterdrop stickers around journaling and on photos..

Use vellum to overlay the background and make journaling legible.

Use an oval template to ensure smooth edges.

Glue a piece of fiber in a wavy line to reinforce the water theme.

Anne and Rascal

WHAT YOU'LL NEED
- Paper cutter
- Scissors or crafts knife
- Black marker
- 8½×11-inch piece of background paper with a subtle pattern, such as gray check (Sandy Lyon)
- Black patterned paper (Daisy D's Paper Co.)
- Black paper
- Coordinating pattern paper for title (Westrim Crafts)
- Alphabet stickers
- Adhesive
- Photos

Two similar photos can tell a story, and using them differently can make the page interesting.

To draw attention to a particular photo, enlarge it dramatically and cut away the unnecessary background. Cut the gray patterned paper into random-size blocks and arrange them with white space between to create a subtle geometric pattern.

Frame the title block with a narrow black border. Place black patterned strips on the top and bottom of the page to keep the photos from floating.

Use stickers for the initial letters in the headline. The freestyle look of these letters allows the remaining letters to be completed in handwriting using a black marking pen.

Colorful initials carry out the artistic look and work well with hand-lettering.

White space subtly breaks up the background pattern.

Enlarge and silhouette a photo for a dramatic effect.

ANNE AND RASCAL DEC '93

The Butterfly Garden

WHAT YOU'LL NEED

- *12-inch squares of green and peach textured paper (Karen Foster Design)*
- *12-inch square of peach speckled paper (Karen Foster Design)*
- *Rubber stamps in daisy, dragonfly, and bee designs (Stampin' Up!)*
- *Ochre ink pad*
- *White card stock*
- *Paper cutter*
- *Decorative-edge scissors*
- *Transfer lettering and ruled embellishments (Letratype)*
- *Die cut butterfly (Deluxe Cuts)*
- *Butterfly stickers (Sticky Pix by Paper House Productions)*
- *Round paper punch*
- *Scissors*
- *Adhesive: photos*

Use a die cut to reinforce the theme of the page.

Stamp subtle designs on the background paper.

Some of the most precious photos are those taken on the sly. These two youngsters were studying the nature around them when the camera captured their fascination.

When using several nature shots, green usually makes a good background. To make a chalklike background even richer, randomly stamp flowers, bees, and dragonflies.

To make a column for journaling, cut a 3½-inch-wide strip from peach paper using decorative-edge scissors. Punch holes as desired. Turn over the remaining (cutaway piece) of paper to reveal the white. Glue on the peach paper strip to repeat the design along the edge. Glue to the background.

Kids are fascinated by bugs, and these candid shots combined with postcard-pretty nature photos capture the magic.

Crop the photos into rectangles and squares, and mat them with narrow white borders. Silhouette a photo. After the arrangement is decided and a column at the right is saved for journaling, place the headline. Draw light pencil rules as guides for a straight headline. The rub-on lettering is applied from the center outward to ensure centering. Place a letter on the drawn line and burnish (rub) the back with a dull pencil until the letter is transferred. The motifs under the headline and at the top of the journaling column are applied in the same manner.

When the photos are in place, add butterfly die cut, stickers, and journaling for a beautiful tribute to nature.

THE BUTTERFLY GARDEN

We found the most beautiful garden on the Saylorville bike trail. The kids were fascinated seeing hundreds of colorful butterflies.

Use rub-ons for the headline and decorative accents.

Trim a journaling strip using decorative-edge scissors and a paper punch.

Turn the remainder of the paper piece over and use this white piece to back the peach paper.

Place butterfly stickers to appear as though in flight or resting on the page.

Penny & Frieda

WHAT YOU'LL NEED
- 12-inch squares of ochre background paper
- Black-and-white swirled-pattern paper (Daisy D's)
- Red star paper
- Pink parchment paper
- Black paper
- Computer and printer
- Tracing paper
- Pencil; pink, black, and white opaque marking pens
- Pinking shears
- Crafts knife
- Paper cutter
- Adhesive: photos

Every family has its own special stories. When recording one of these stories in your scrapbook, consider writing your journaling as a story or as a poem to add to the creativity of your page. This was one such story told on these two pages with a few photographs and a poem written by the owner of the pets. Because the story was told in detail, no photo captions are needed.

The background color has special meaning here. Not only does it complement the photos, it is the same color as Penny the beloved chicken. A simple color can trigger fond memories and evoke happy emotions. To create a poem as journaling, type it on a computer and print it on colored paper.

Use opaque markers to create a colorful headline.

Enlarge and crop one main photo for this page.

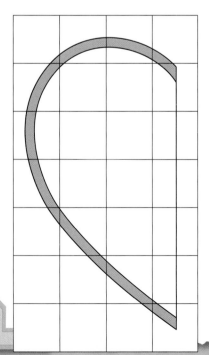

HEART MAT
PATTERN

1 SQUARE =
1 INCH

*Whether you have pets in love or kids with
their heads in the clouds, this whimsical layout is a sure fit.*

To mimic this layout, use only two patterned papers to mount photos and cut out hearts.

To make the heart mat or accent hearts, use the patterns, *opposite* and *below*, enlarging the mat pattern 200 percent. Cut out the shapes and transfer the designs to printed papers. To make the large heart mat, cut a 6½-inch square from black swirl paper using pinking shears. Turn the square on point and trace the larger heart. Cut out with a crafts knife. Cut the inner mat using the small mat heart pattern. Trim to fit behind the black mat.

Cut the smaller hearts from pink paper and black papers. Adhere the pink over the black.

Create a variety of smaller hearts using layers of papers. Outline with a marking pen.

To make a handwritten headline, use opaque marking pens. Start with black, then layer with pink and white, allowing some of the black to show at the bottom and left side of each letter to create a shadow.

Cut out paper hearts using the patterns below.

Trim all photo mats the same size for consistency.

Write a poem for extra-interesting journaling.

This is a story of two creatures, a tale rarely heard of

about the foul and the feline who truly fell in love.

The Calico they called Frieda, the copper colored chicken named Penney.

There were cats and dogs and ducks and geese, so they were just two of many.

But somehow there was something strange within the air.

Before too long these two pets became a perfect pair.

They never ever parted and did everything together...

wind, snow, rain or shine any kind of weather.

They began to adapt, each to the other.

Their habits were confused with the species of another.

Penney learned to hunt the fields for rodent prey.

They were often seen on the horizon in the middle of the day.

And in the evening when Penny roosted in her tree,

you could look 3 feet below and sleeping Frieda you would see.

They soon became the item among the animals on the farm.

They were known by many because of their unusual charm.

They had been in the field one day hunting rodents and eating corn.

Penny met her tragic end then and all our hearts were torn.

She didn't understand the road that divided the field from her yard.

The truck came rushing by and for a second let down her guard.

We're thankful for the time we had with our two beloved friends.

The story was strange and sweet, and sadly this is where it ends.

HEART ACCENT PATTERNS

Fishing Kids

WHAT YOU'LL NEED
- *Light mottled green paper*
- *Contrasting paper to mount photos*
- *Paper cutter or crafts knife*
- *Soft blue chalk*
- *Red and white paper*
- *Opaque marking pens in black, red, and white*
- *Scissors*
- *Adhesive*
- *Photos*

BOBBER PATTERN

Create easy freehand journaling with a black marking pen. Go over with a white opaque marking pen, leaving a black shadow on bottom and left.

Tilt photos at various angles to add to the whimsy of the page.

This early spring day was a most memorable time for these four siblings at their uncle's pond. This whimsical layout combines a little animated drawing with photos to portray the fun of the day.

The subtle green background complements the colors in the photos without competing with them. This green is also similar to the color of the pond, another element that triggers that happy memory.

The little girl in the upper left deliberately breaks out of her photo box and is placed in that spot to move your eye around the page and to the right.

Matthew→

Hailey↑

all our fish→

Cassie←

Jacob→

You can almost hear "I got one! I got one!" with these exciting pages that grab you hook, line, and sinker.

The fishing line naturally carries your eye over. Extra closeup photos, such as the pile of fish, add emphasis to the topic.

Trim each photo and mount on colored paper. Crop the photos to emphasize the subject. Notice two of these have partial silhouetted areas. This and the completely silhouetted fish in the lower right make interesting shapes and encourage eye movement from left to right.

Create the bobber, hook, and worm by tracing the patterns, *opposite* and *right*, onto white paper. Color the pieces using the pattern as a guide. Cut out the shapes. Add blue chalk near the large fish silhouette. Draw in white bubbles.

For the journaling, use a black marking pen and write over it with a white opaque marking pen.

HOOK AND WORM
PATTERN

Be sure to include all the participants when telling a fishing tale.

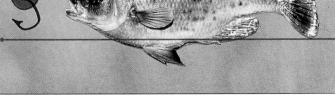

Silhouette an image that depicts the theme.

Scrape blue chalk with a crafts knife and blend in the dust with a cotton ball to create a water effect.

Dad's Garden

WHAT YOU'LL NEED

- *12-inch squares of background paper (Colorbök)*
- *Paper cutter*
- *Corner rounder*
- *Colored papers for borders*
- *Green marking pen*
- *Yellow tube-style paint*
- *Decorative-edge scissors*
- *Adhesive*
- *Photos*

This father's garden is truly a work of art, and the photographs portray the beauty. The painterly green background paper accentuates the color in gorgeous outdoor photos.

To choose mat colors, take your photos to the scrapbook store and select colors that work with each photo. This layout uses four mat colors. Pick a color from the photograph that appears in it but that is not necessarily the prominent color. For example, green is the dominant color in the photo of the peonies and dogs in the upper left on the right-hand page. However, mauve paper was chosen to match the vibrant color of the peonies. Selecting paper colors using this rule will bring out the color in your photos.

Create a focal point using one large vertical photo with double matting.

Use decorative-edge scissors to cut strips of color for emphasis.

Cover dead space in a photograph with a small interesting inset.

*Capture the beauty of a garden in full bloom to enjoy
and remember every season of the year.*

To soften the look of each photo, use a corner rounder. To spice up large uninteresting areas in photos, add a photo inset, such as the orange poppies at the bottom of the large vertical photo.

Add journaling in a marking pen that is slightly darker than the background paper so it doesn't distract from the many photos. To create the headline, first write the title in green marking pen. Highlight and add dimension by writing over the letters using yellow dimensional paint.

Coordinate mat colors with something from the photo.

Use green journaling for legibility without distracting from the colorful photos.

Round the photo corners for a delicate look.

Classic Cars

WHAT YOU'LL NEED

- 12-inch squares of silver gray background paper
- Black paper
- Red metallic adhesive-backed paper
- Computer and printer
- Scissors
- Crafts knife
- Black dimensional paint pen
- Adhesive
- Photos

This is an arrangement of many favorite photos taken at a car show. Quite a few photos are arranged in an organized fashion to look neat and interesting.

To simplify several photos of details, organize them onto panels matted with black. Silhouetted items, such as the top row of cars, work better on a busy layout when they appear in one area.

The main photo of the couple gets attention as the focal point. To draw attention like this, silhouette a large bold photo. The bold panels on the left and right, along with the headline, draw your eye from left to right and to the main photo.

To make the headline, type the words on a computer. Use a mirror setting on your computer so that when you print the

Group detail shots to make an organized layout.

Back detail shots with a solid paper color for unity.

Closeup details make this scrapbook spread a car-lover's dream.
Taken at a car show, these photos recall several vintage beauties.

headline it reads backward. Print the headline. Cut and peel off a section of vinyl large enough to apply to the back of the printed headline.

Trim the words closely with scissors. Apply adhesive to the paper side and affix the words to the layout.

Add additional journaling using a black paint pen. When you deal with a lot of photos, as illustrated here, keep the journaling to a minimum.

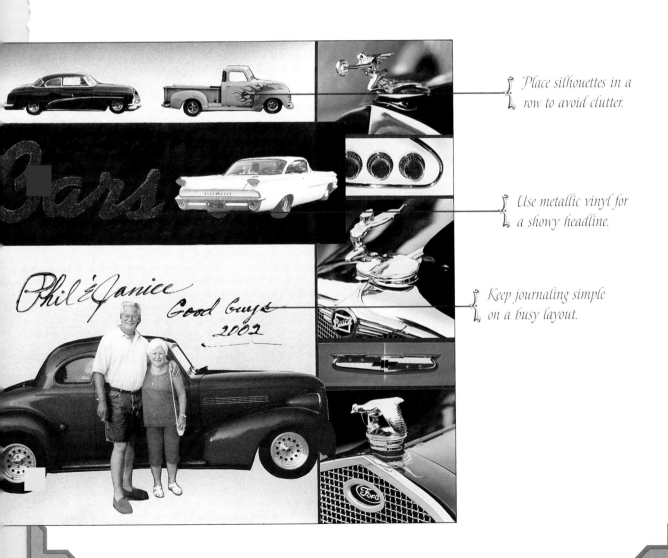

Place silhouettes in a row to avoid clutter.

Use metallic vinyl for a showy headline.

Keep journaling simple on a busy layout.

A Day at the Hangar

WHAT YOU'LL NEED
- Two 12-inch squares of cloud background paper (Frances Meyer)
- Red and white paper
- Paper cutter
- Crafts knife
- Decorative-edge scissors
- Red marking pen
- Lettering stencil
- Adhesive
- Photos

The children in these photos will remember how fascinating it was to visit Dad at his workplace when they see these pages years from now. Whether you own a plane or you're taking the kids on their first airplane ride, this is a quick and simple design.

This arrangement uses only a few elements. The background of perfect white fluffy clouds is soft enough to give importance to the photos and perfect to combine with the silhouetted plane.

To achieve this look, trim each photo to eliminate uninteresting space and to focus on the main person. Different sizes and shapes of photos will work very well in the right arrangement. This

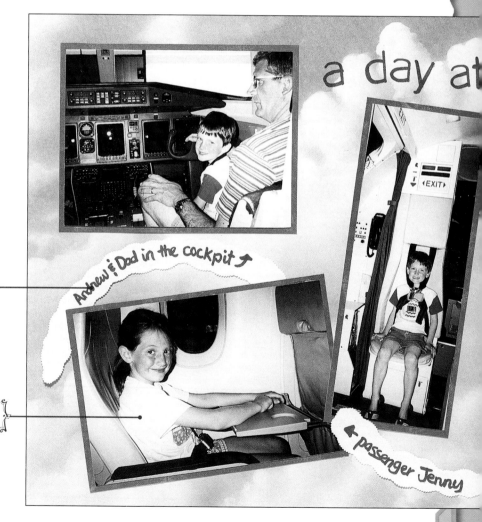

Write journaling in red on white paper and cut with scalloped scissors.

The position of faces, arrangement of shapes, and curvy line help the flow of this layout.

a day at

Andrew & Dad in the cockpit →

← passenger Jenny

Whether dad's a pilot or you're off on your first airborne vacation, this arrangement is a hit for those high-in-the-sky moments.

arrangement is informal and has a lot of movement appropriate to the topic. The two vertical pieces balance the horizontal shapes, and the continuous curvy journaling line carries the eye easily from left to right.

You may have some photos that are not overly colorful but are interesting. The most noticeable color in these was the small amount of red shown in the woman's clothing, so red was chosen as the accent color. Frame all photos using a consistent mat color. Use the same color to write the journaling.

Overlap photos to cover uninteresting areas. The plane in the sky was photographed in the hangar. And while the photograph

was drab, grainy, and out of focus, cutting away the dark background and placing it in the sky allowed it to be used.

the hangar with dad

Dad's Plane →

← attendant Mom ↑

Create a headline with a stencil and marking pen.

Silhouette items to add to the composition.

Cloud paper is the perfect choice for pages with an airplane theme.

ADHESIVES
Aleenes
duncancrafts.com

Centis
Centis Consumer Products Division
888/236-8476

Elmer's Glue Stick
800/848-9400
elmers.com
comments@elmers.com

Suze Weinberg Design Studio
732/761-2400
732/761-2410 (fax)
Suzenj@aol.com

Tombow USA
800/835-3232
tombowusa.com

BRADS
Magic Scraps
972/238-1838
magicscraps.com

BUTTONS
Le Bouton Buttons
Blumenthal Lansing Co.
563/538-4211
563/538-4243 (fax)
sales@buttonsplus.com

DIE CUTS
Cock A Doodle
800/262-9727
cockadoodle.com

Deluxe Cuts
480/497-9005
707/922-2175 (fax)
deluxecuts.com

Fresh Cuts
Rebecca Sower
EK Success Ltd.
eksuccess.com

Griff's Shortcuts
989/894-5916
griffs-shortcuts.com

Little Extras
361/814-9191
littleextrasdiecuts.com

Stamping Station
801/444-3838
stampingstation.com

EYELETS
Persnippity
801/523-3338
persnippity.com

FIBER
Cut-It-Up
530/389-2233
cut-it-up.com

FOAM SQUARES
Therm O Web
800/323-0799

**OPAQUE WRITERS/
WATERPROOF MARKERS**
EK Success Ltd.
eksuccess.com
(Wholesale only. Available at most
crafts stores.)

PHOTOGRAPHIC IMAGES
Shotz Photo Papers by Danelle
    Johnson
Creative Imaginations, Inc.
cigift.com

PRESS-ON GEMS
Stampa Rosa, Inc.
707/527-8267
stamparosa.com

**PROFESSIONAL
PHOTOGRAPHY**
Andy Lyons Cameraworks
304 15th Street
Des Moines, IA 50309
515/244-9001
515/244-3146 (fax)
(scrapbook pages 56–57)

Images of Iowa
Jolene M. Rosauer
801 10th Street
Grundy Center, IA 50638
319/825-4045
images@gemuni.net
(scrapbook pages 144–145)

Roy Meronek
1821 Iowa Avenue
Superior, WI 54880
715/392-8689
(scrapbook page 31)

Virginia Mickunas
(scrpabook pages 124–125)

PROTECTIVE SLEEVES
Westrim Crafts
888/727-2727

RUBBER STAMPS/INK PADS
Art Impressions
800/393-2014
artimpressions.com

Stampin' Up!
801/601-5400
stampinup.com

**SCISSORS, PUNCHES &
ROUNDERS**
Creative Memories
800/341-5275
creativememories.com

Fiskars Scissors
608/259-1649
fiskars.com

Emagination Crafts, Inc.
866/238-9770
service@emaginationcraftsinc.com

EK Success Ltd.
eksuccess.com
(Wholesale only. Available at most
crafts stores.)

SCRAPBOOK PAPERS
All My Memories
888/553-1998

Anna Griffin
404/817-8170 (phone)
404/817-0590 (fax)
annagriffin.com

Art Accents
360/733-8989
artaccents.net

Bazzill Basics Paper
480/558-8557
bazzillbasics.com

Colorbök
800/366-4660
colorbok.com

Daisy D's Paper Co.
801/447-8955
daisydspaper.com

DMD, Inc.
800/805-9890

Doodlebug
801/966-9952

Family Archives
888/622-6556
heritagescrapbooks.com

Frances Meyer, Inc.
800/372-6237
francesmeyer.com

Hot Off The Press, Inc.
800/227-9595
paperpizazz.com

Karen Foster Design, Inc.
karenfosterdesign.com

Making Memories
800/286-5263
makingmemories.com

Memories Forever
Westrim Crafts
800/727-2727
westrimcrafts.com

The Paper Loft
866/254-1961 (toll free)
paperloft.com
(Wholesale only. Available at most
crafts stores.)

Pixie Press
888/834-2883
pixiepress.com

Plaid Enterprises, Inc.
800/842-4197
plaidonline.com

Provo Craft
provocraft.com
(Wholesale only. Available at most
crafts stores.)

Sandylion
800/387-4215
905/475-0523 (International)
sandylion.com

Scrap-ease What's New, Ltd.
800/272-3874
480/832-2928 (fax)
whatsnewltd.com

Sweetwater
14711 Road 15
Fort Morgan, CO 80701
970/867-4428

Westrim Crafts
800/727-2727

Wübie Prints
wubieprints.com
(Wholesale only. Available at most
crafts stores.)

Two Busy Moms
800/272-4794
TwoBusyMoms.com

STICKERS
Canson
800/628-9283
canson-us.com

The Gifted Line
John Grossman, Inc.
310/390-9900

Highsmith
800/558-3899
highsmith.com

K & Co.
816/389-4150
KandCompany.com

me & my BIG ideas
949/589-4607
meandmybigideas.com

Mrs. Grossman's Paper Co.
800/429-4549
mrsgrossmans.com

Once Upon A Scribble
702/896-2181
onceuponascribble.com

Paper Punch
800/397-2737

Paper House Productions
800/255-7316
paperhouseproductions.com

SRM Press
800/323-9589
srmpress.com
(Wholesale only. Available at most
crafts stores.)

Stickopotamus
P.O. Box 1047
Clifton, NJ 07014-1047
973/594-0540 (fax)
stickopotamus.com

RUB-ON LETTERING
AND MOTIFS
Chartpak, Inc.
800/628-1910
800/762-7918 (fax)
chartpak.com

The Paper Patch
www.paperpatch.com
(Wholesale only. Available at most
crafts stores.)

Scrapbook Borders
scrapbookborders.com

WIRE MESH
ScrapYard 329
775/829-1118
scrapyard329.com

index

DESIGNERS

Susan Banker—30–32, 40–42, 44–45, 56–57, 68–69, 80–83, 86–89, 91, 96–100, 102–103, 118–119, 126–127, 130–131, 144–145.

Carol Dahlstrom—39, 63, 70, 74–75, 111.

Phyllis Dobbs—28.

Phyllis Dunstan—46–47, 104–105, 133.

Kellie Gould—117.

Dawn Johnson—38, 43, 50, 52–55, 110, 120–121, 132.

Tammy Kempf—90, 114–115.

Diane Reams—48–49.

Emily Robidoux—60–61.

Cheri Thieleke—84–85, 106–107, 128, 142.

Alice Wetzel—29, 33–37, 51, 62, 64–67, 72–73, 92–95, 101, 116, 124–125, 129, 136–141, 143, 146–155.

EXCLUSIVE PAPER DESIGNERS

Susan Banker—181, 183, 187, 189.

Alice Wetzel—161, 163, 165, 167, 169, 171, 173, 175, 177, 179, 185, 191.

PHOTOSTYLING

Carol Dahlstrom

Donna Chesnut, assistant

SPECIAL THANKS TO

Memory Bound Scrapbook Store

641 N. Ankeny Blvd.

Ankeny, IA 50021

515/965-1102

www.memorybound.com

Photography Experts:

    Andy Lyons Cameraworks

    Peter Krumhardt

    Scott Little

How to Use Our Papers

The acid-free papers on the following pages have been designed to use in your own scrapbook projects. You'll find never-seen-before background papers, borders, mats, accents, cutouts, labels, journaling boxes—all ready for you to photocopy and use as is or any way you wish.

CREATE YOUR OWN PAGES USING OUR EXCLUSIVE PAPERS ON PAGES 161-191.

To see how we've used the papers, the page reference is noted on the back of each paper. Accompanying each of these scrapbook pages are specific instructions to re-create the page, including the percentages used to reduce or enlarge the original papers. You can reduce, enlarge, or combine these art elements as desired to fit your photos and complete your pages. Keep in mind, if using a paper or accent for a 12-inch-square page and you want it to reach top to bottom, you must enlarge it (the book pages aren't quite that big!). Another option is adhering the pages to 12-inch-square or or other desired size background papers.

To assist when cropping sections from the full patterned pages, we've provided a $\frac{1}{4}$-inch grid on the back.

To photocopy a paper, carefully remove the page from the book along the perforated line. Permission for photocopying the page for personal use is noted on the back of each paper.

The paper you photocopy onto depends on how you use each design. For example, for a heavy background paper, use card stock. If the photocopied item is a cutout accent, journaling box, or photo mat, use standard paper.

Some photocopy centers can alter the color when copying, others cannot. When making multiple copies, always check the first copy of a page and either approve it or ask to correct the color. In a situation where a copy machine color is not acceptable, ask for the color to be adjusted to better reflect the original.

Once the page is photocopied, you can trim it using a crafts knife, paper cutter, or scissors to create meaningful pages for your next scrapbook project. When silhouetting elements, move the photo or paper piece (rather than the scissors) and a neater trim will result.

So have fun using these exclusive papers and make your scrapbook pages shine with creativity!

ALTERNATE
JOURNAL BOX

JOURNAL
BOX

PICTURE MAT

ALTERNATE PHOTO MAT CORNERS

ALTERNATE PHOTO
MAT STRIPS

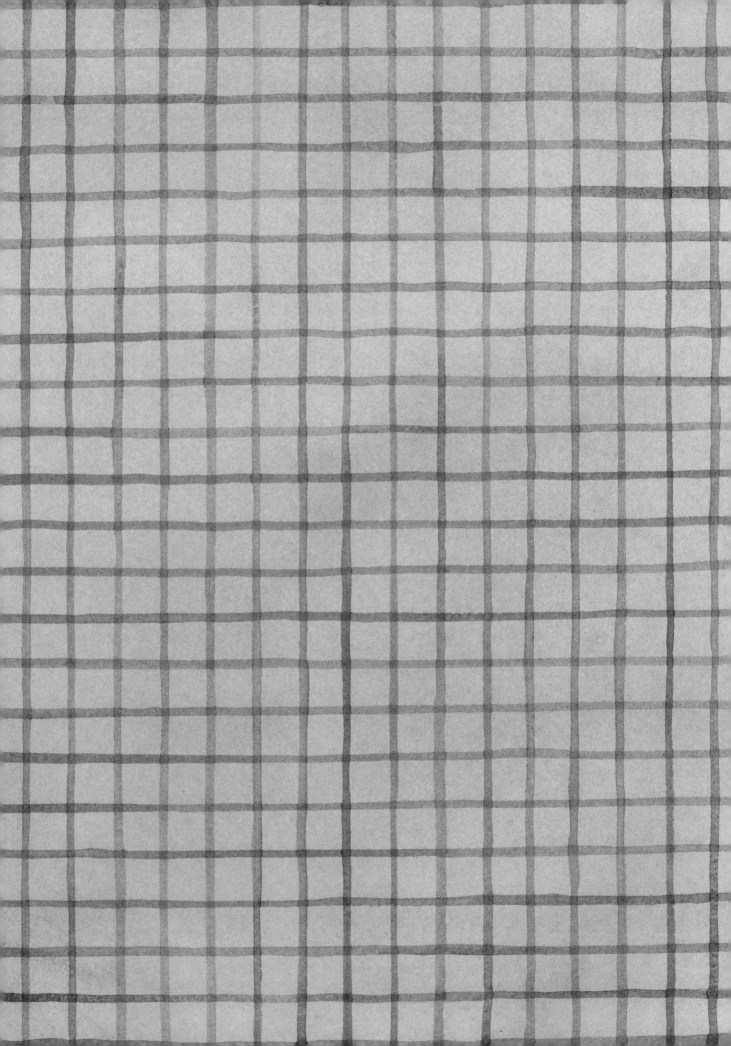

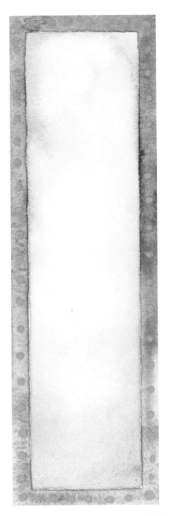

FULL-SIZE JOURNAL BOX

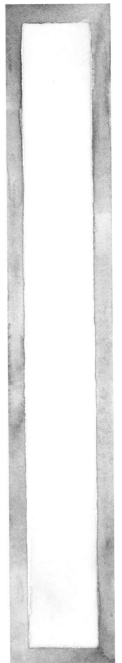

ALTERNATE
JOURNAL BOX

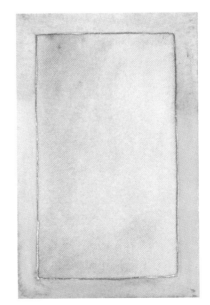

ALTERNATE JOURNAL BOX

FULL-SIZE ACCENTS

VINE BORDERS
enlarge 111% for a 12-inch-square page

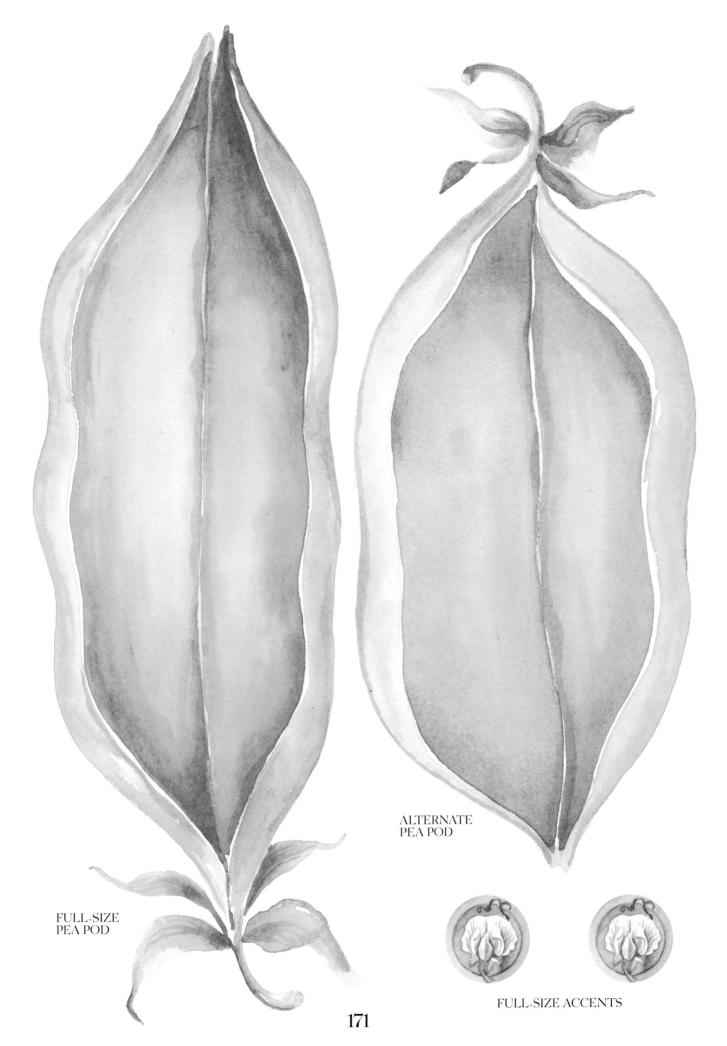

FULL-SIZE
PEA POD

ALTERNATE
PEA POD

FULL-SIZE ACCENTS

171

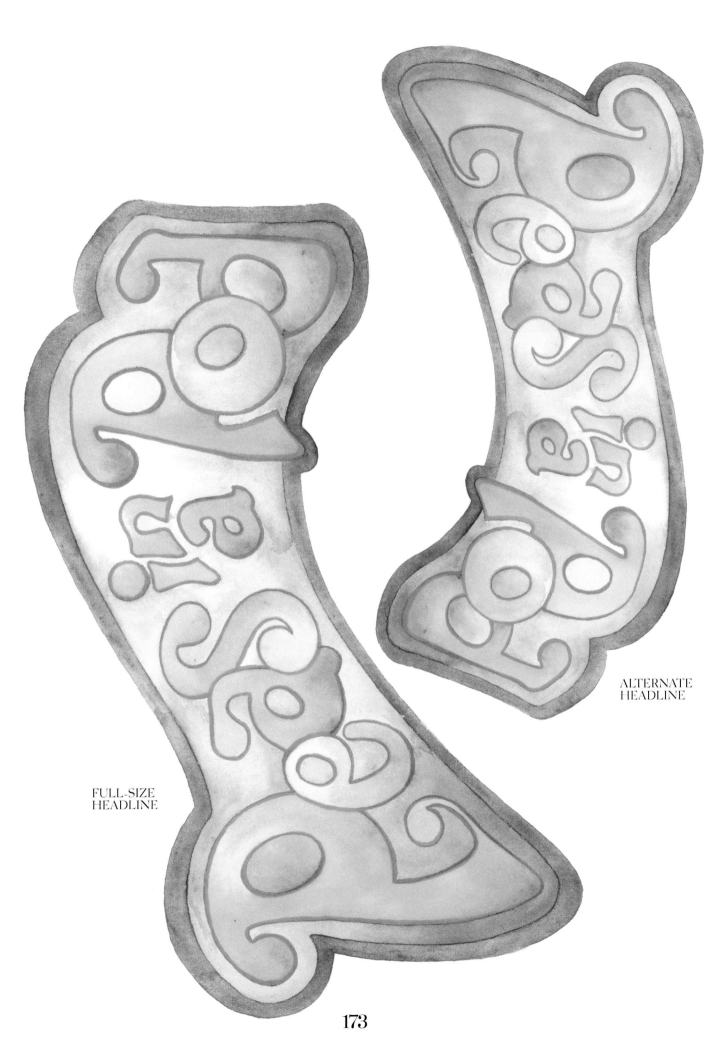

FULL-SIZE
HEADLINE

ALTERNATE
HEADLINE

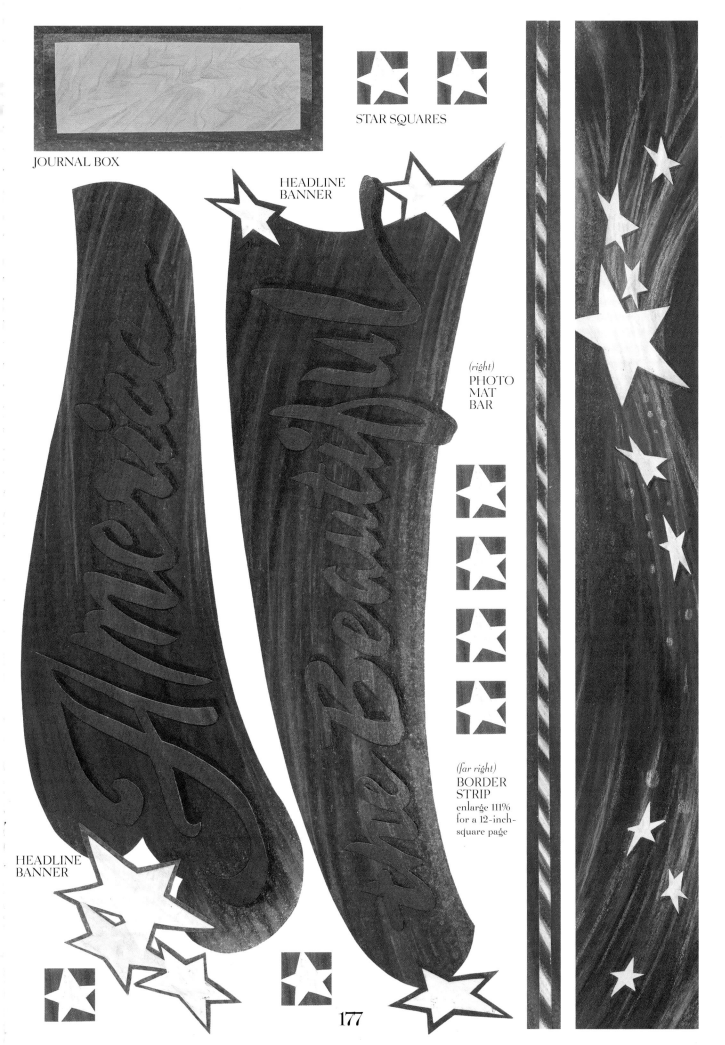

JOURNAL BOX

STAR SQUARES

HEADLINE
BANNER

(right)
PHOTO
MAT
BAR

HEADLINE
BANNER

(far right)
BORDER
STRIP
enlarge 111%
for a 12-inch-
square page

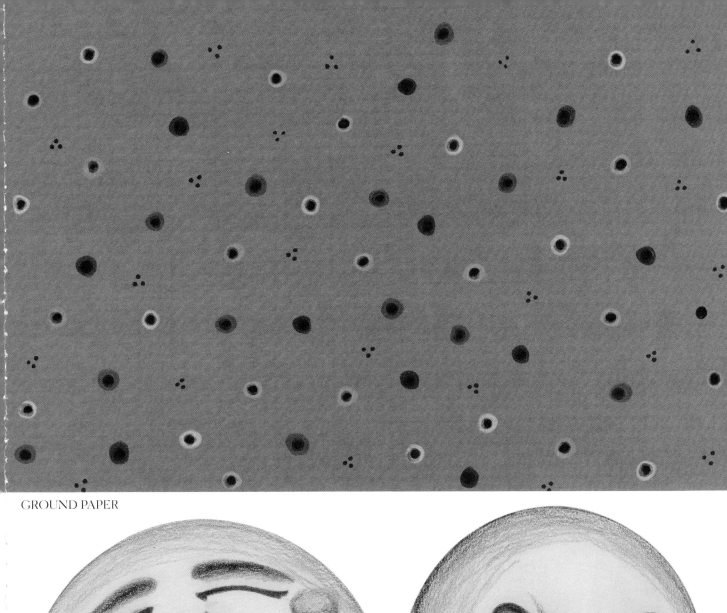

GROUND PAPER

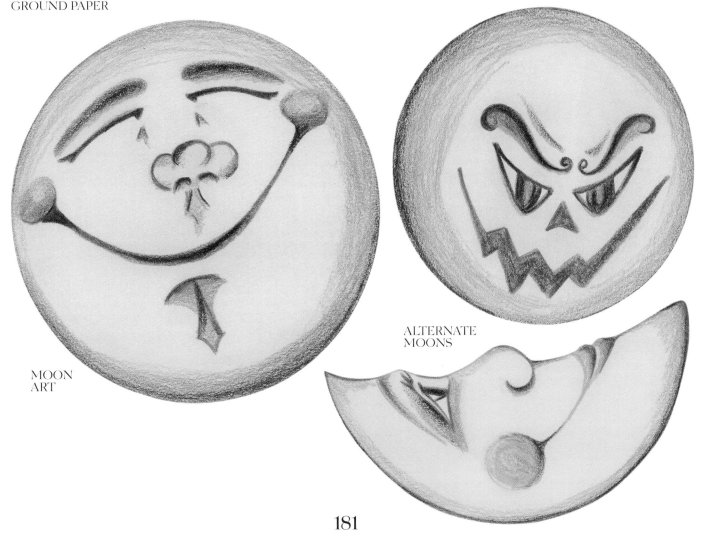

MOON
ART

ALTERNATE
MOONS

181

GRADUATION DAY

PHOTO MAT AND LABEL ELEMENTS

PHOTO MAT

Congratulations!

PHOTO MAT AND JOURNAL BOXES

This certifies that

_____

_____

has satisfactorily completed
the course of study for graduation
on this day of

_____

CERTIFICATE FOR PERSONALIZATION

Marriage Certificate

THIS IS TO CERTIFY

That _____
_____ in the State of _____
and _____ of _____
in the State of _____ were by me joined together in

HOLY MATRIMONY

on the _____ day of _____
in _____

Witness: _____
_____

MARRIAGE CERTIFICATE — Make three photocopies: For the photo mat on the right-hand page, enlarge to 140%; for the vertical floral bands, the headline, and the cutout flowers, enlarge to 220%; and for the certificate to personalize on the left-hand page, reduce to 67%.

187

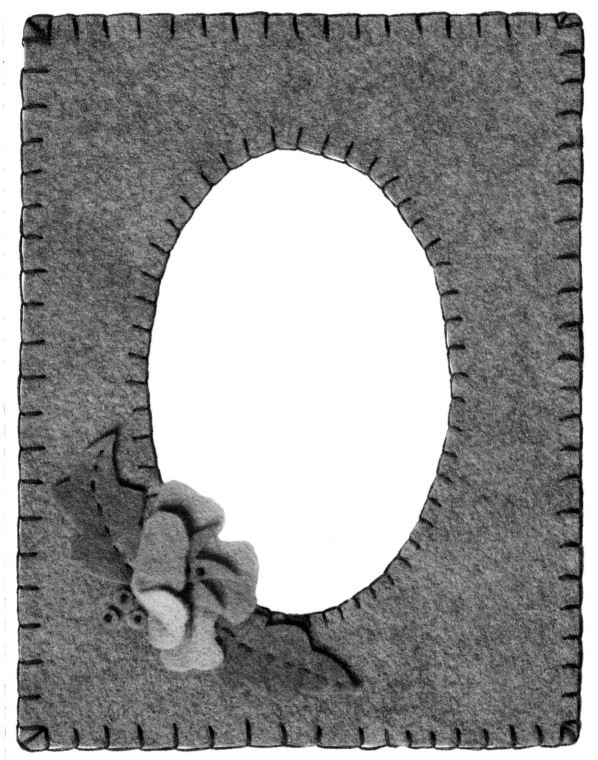

PHOTO MAT

POLKA-DOT TRIANGLES

POLKA-DOT BANDS

PHOTO MAT AND
JOURNAL BOX

HEADLINE *(left)*

PHOTO MATS AND JOURNAL BOX

191